Fairy Sightings

Through the Seasons

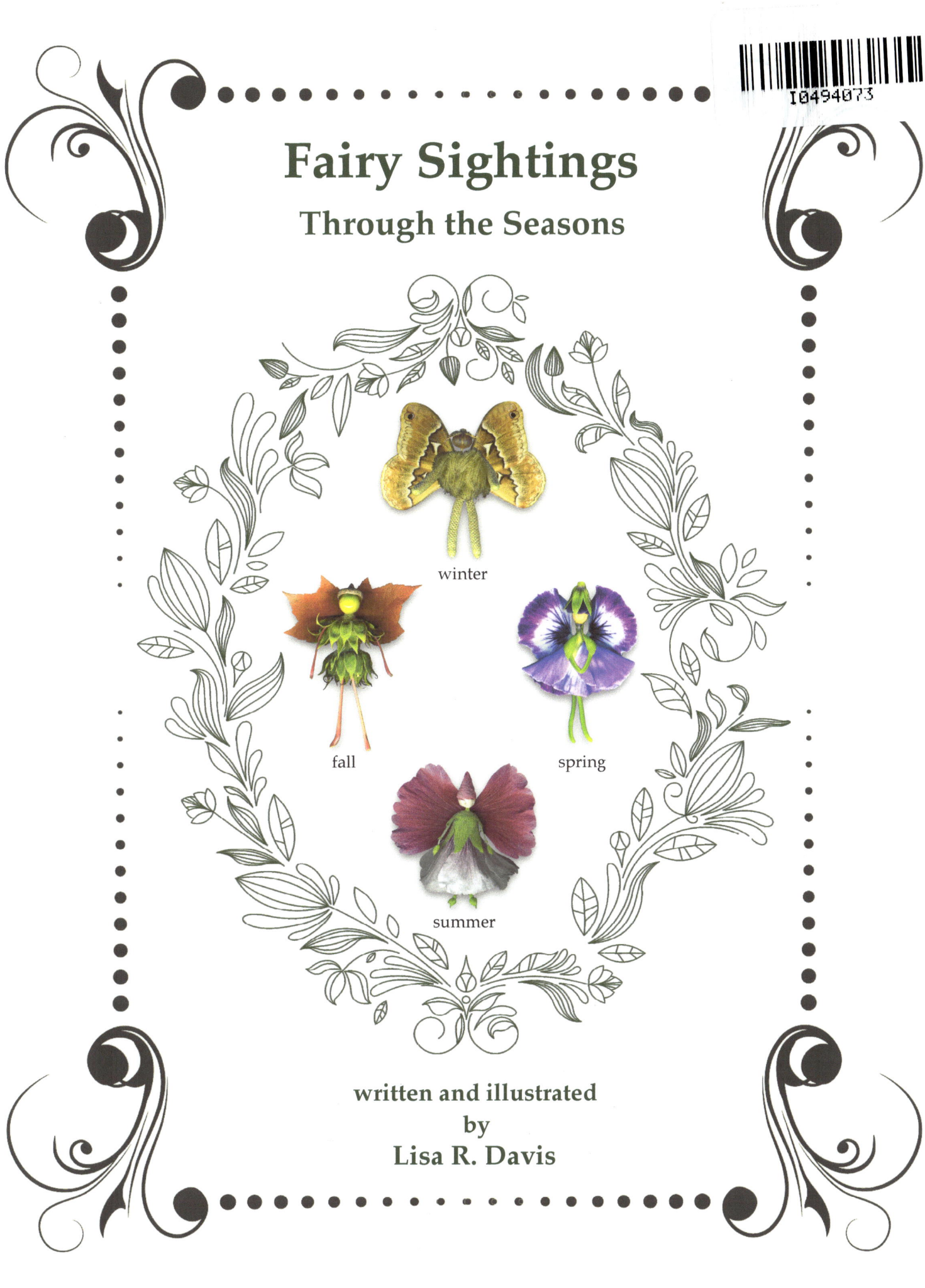

winter

fall

spring

summer

written and illustrated
by
Lisa R. Davis

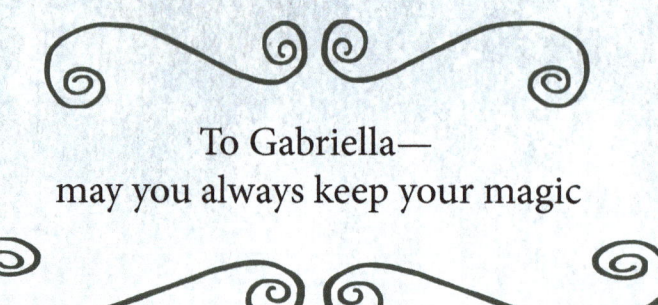

To Gabriella—
may you always keep your magic

Also by Lisa R. Davis
Fairies In My Flowerbeds
Fairies In Spring Flowers
Fairies in Summer

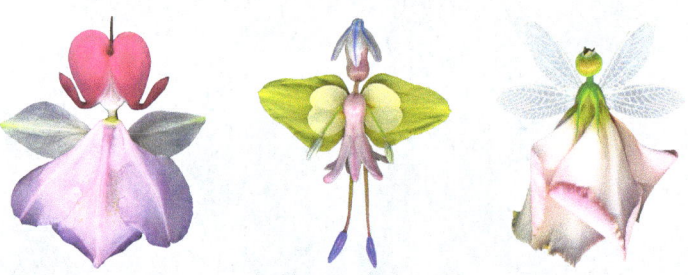

ISBN-13: 978-0692610756
ISBN-10: 0692610758

Winter—
A New Year Begins…

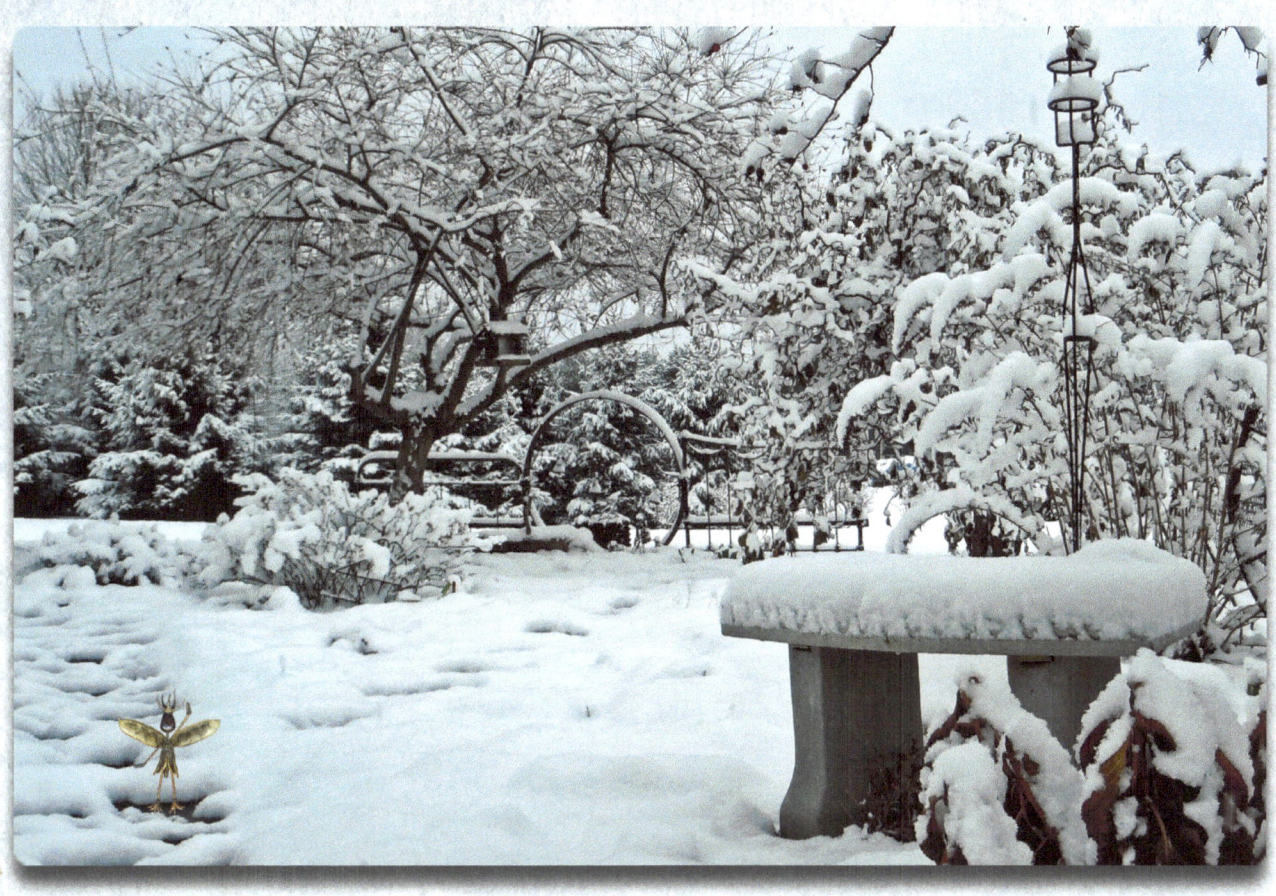

Most plants take a winter break
but nature fairies stay awake.

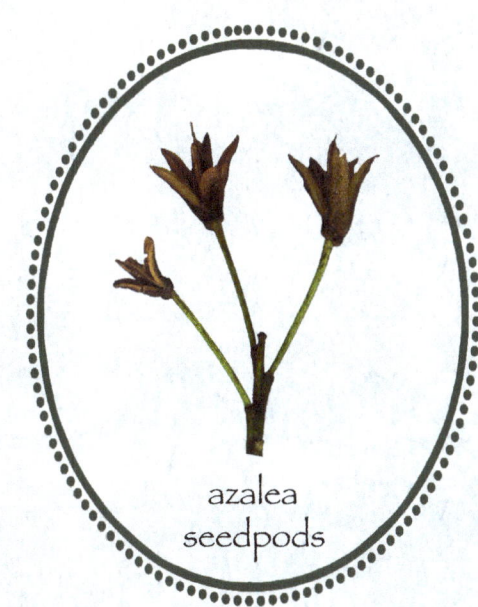

azalea
seedpods

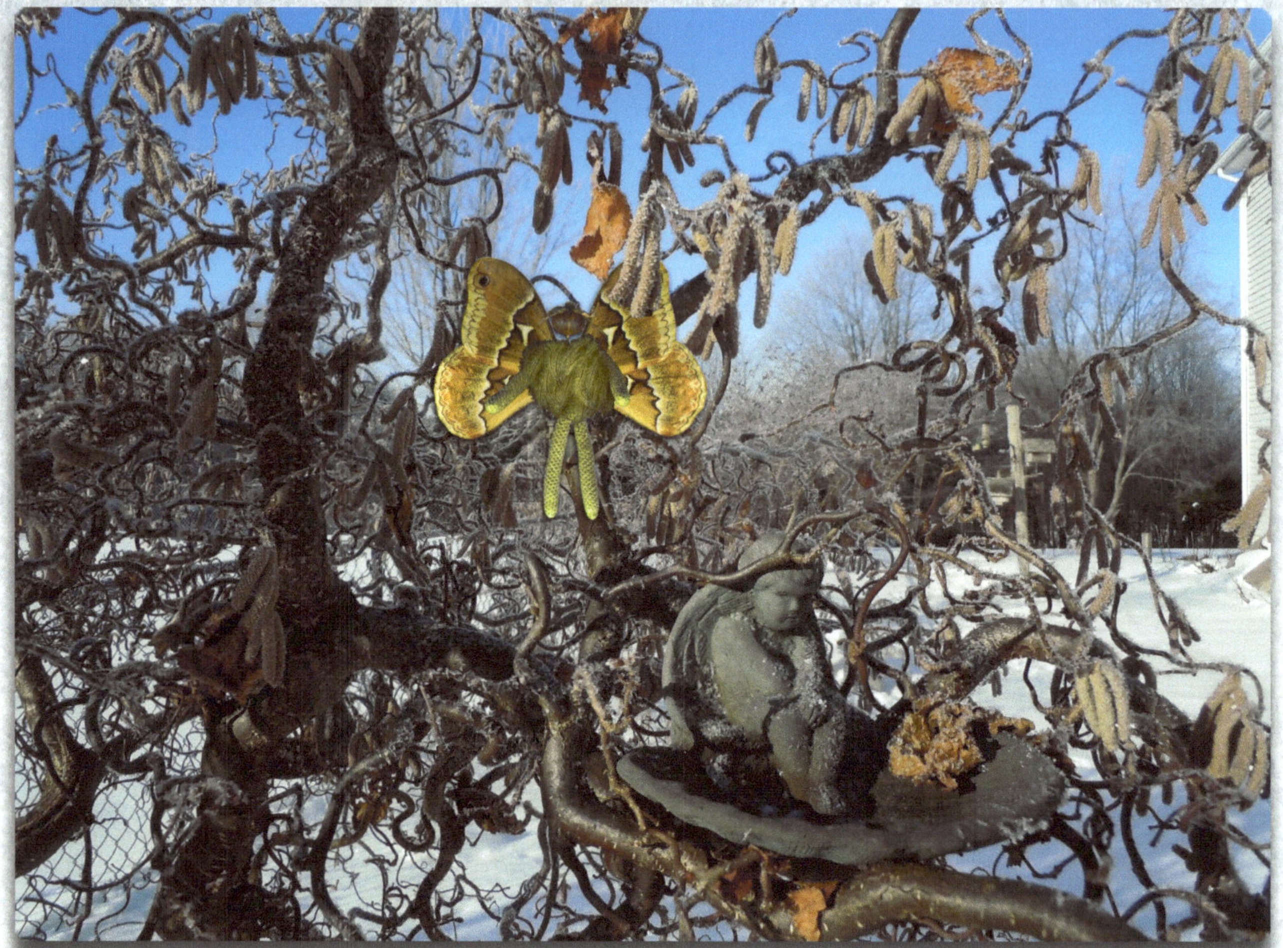

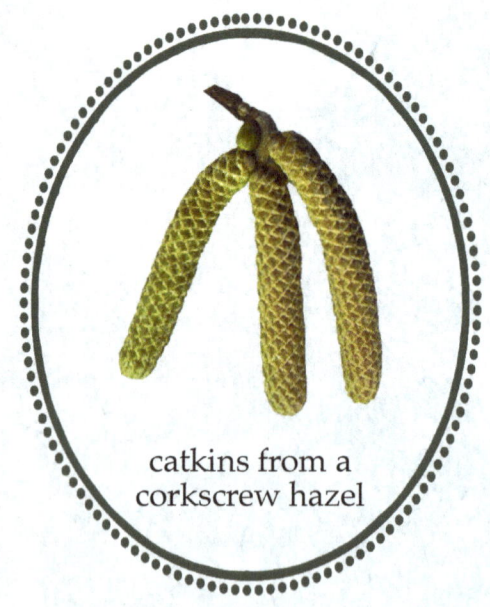

Look around and you may see
a fairy-man in a tree.

catkins from a
corkscrew hazel

The holly bush is shining bright.
Look — a fairy girl in flight!

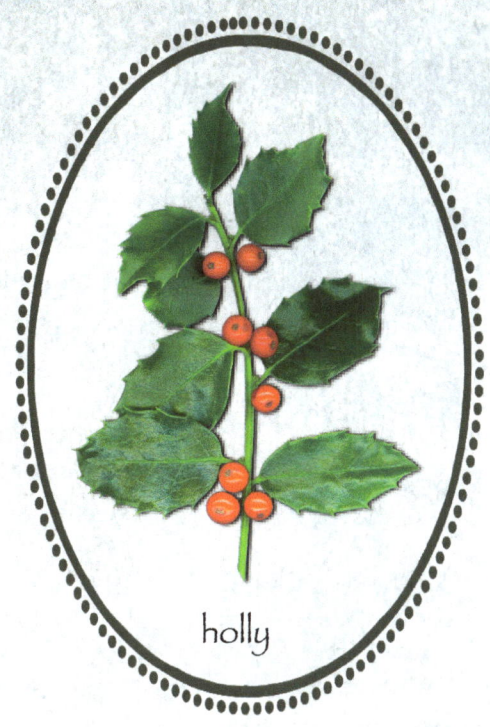

holly

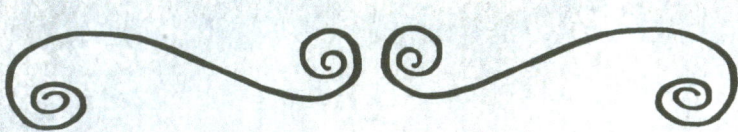

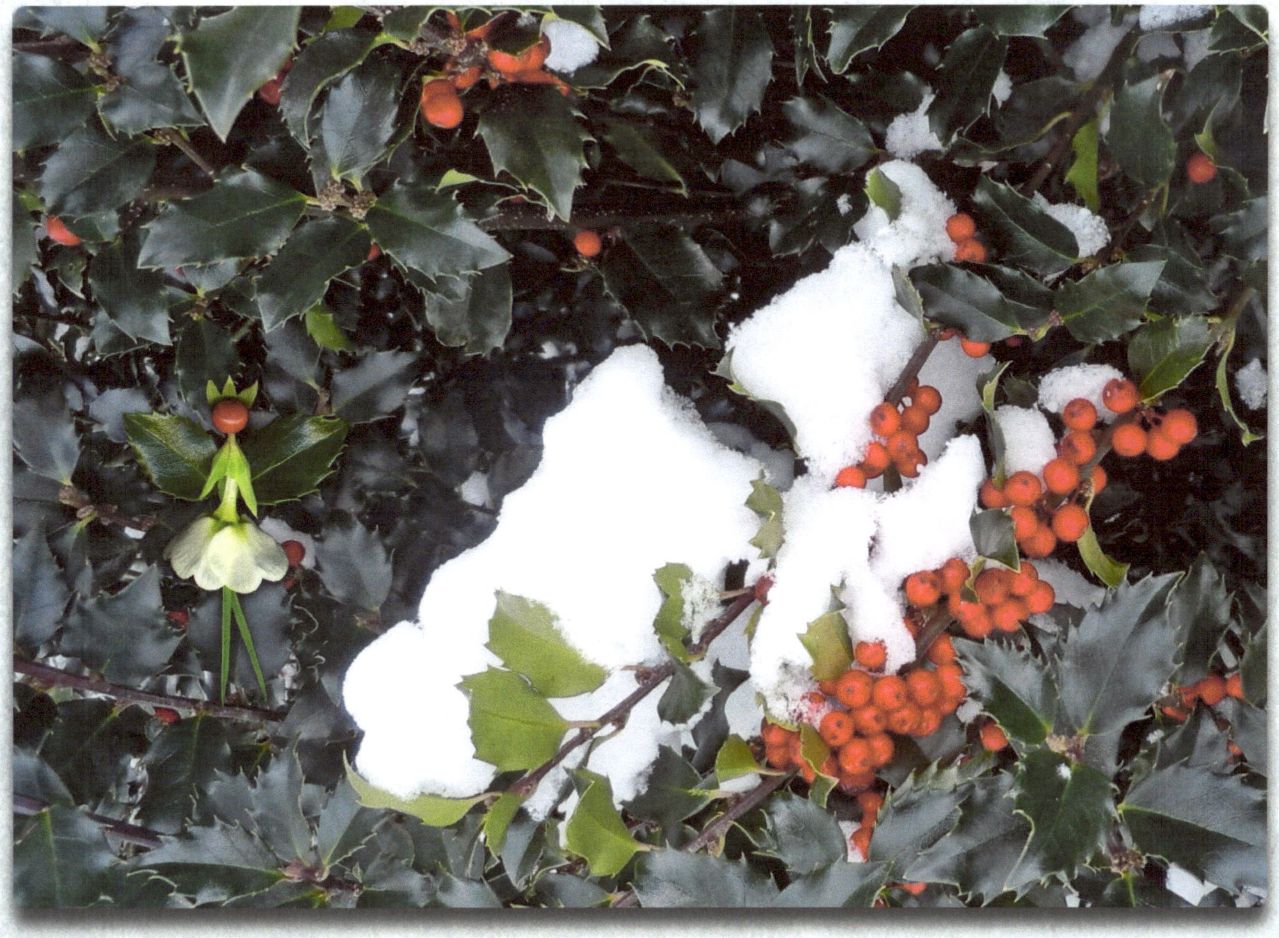

Winter Cycles To Spring

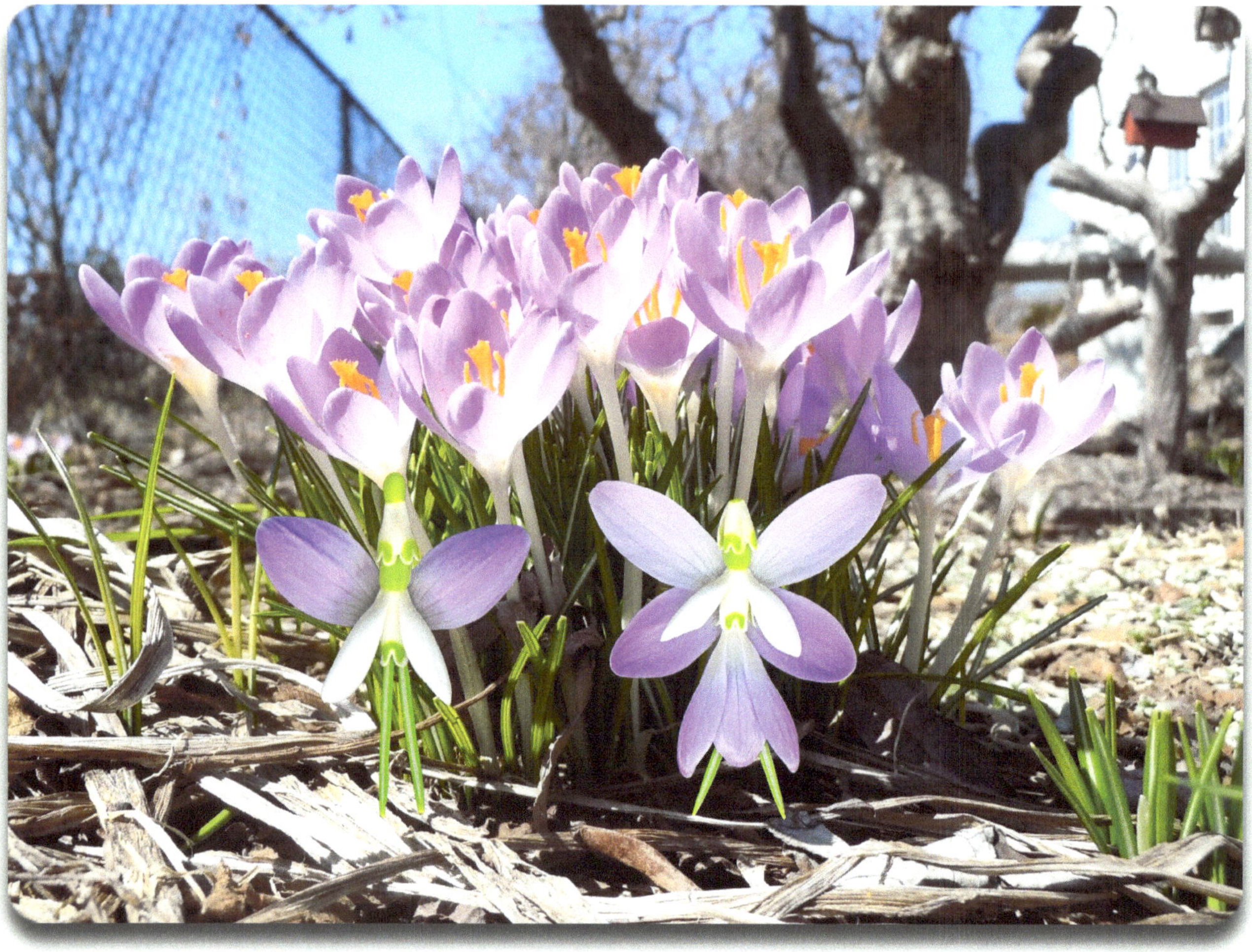

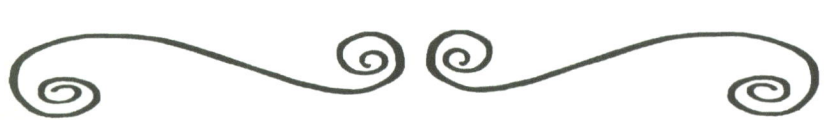

Up through earth spring flowers poke,
used for clothes by fairy folk.

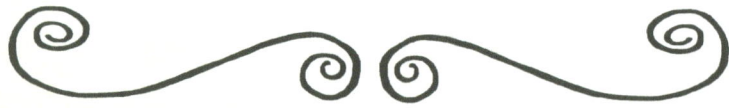

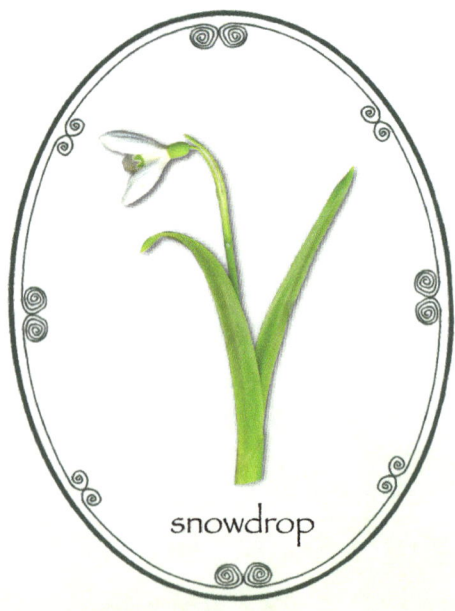

snowdrop

In this shaded garden nook,
someone's hiding. Take a look.

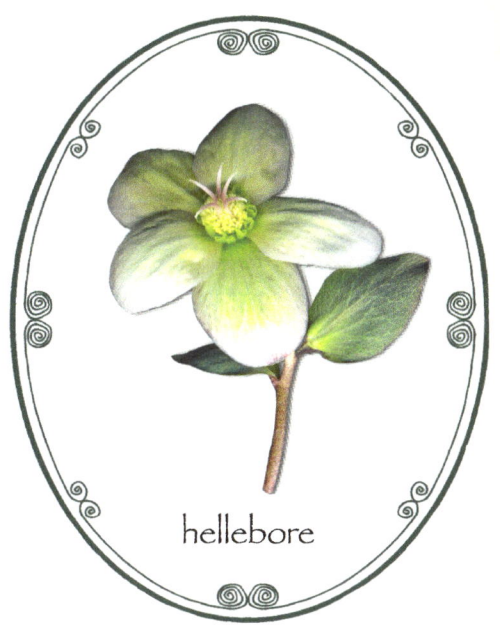

hellebore

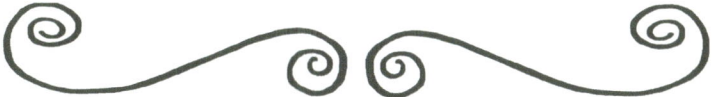

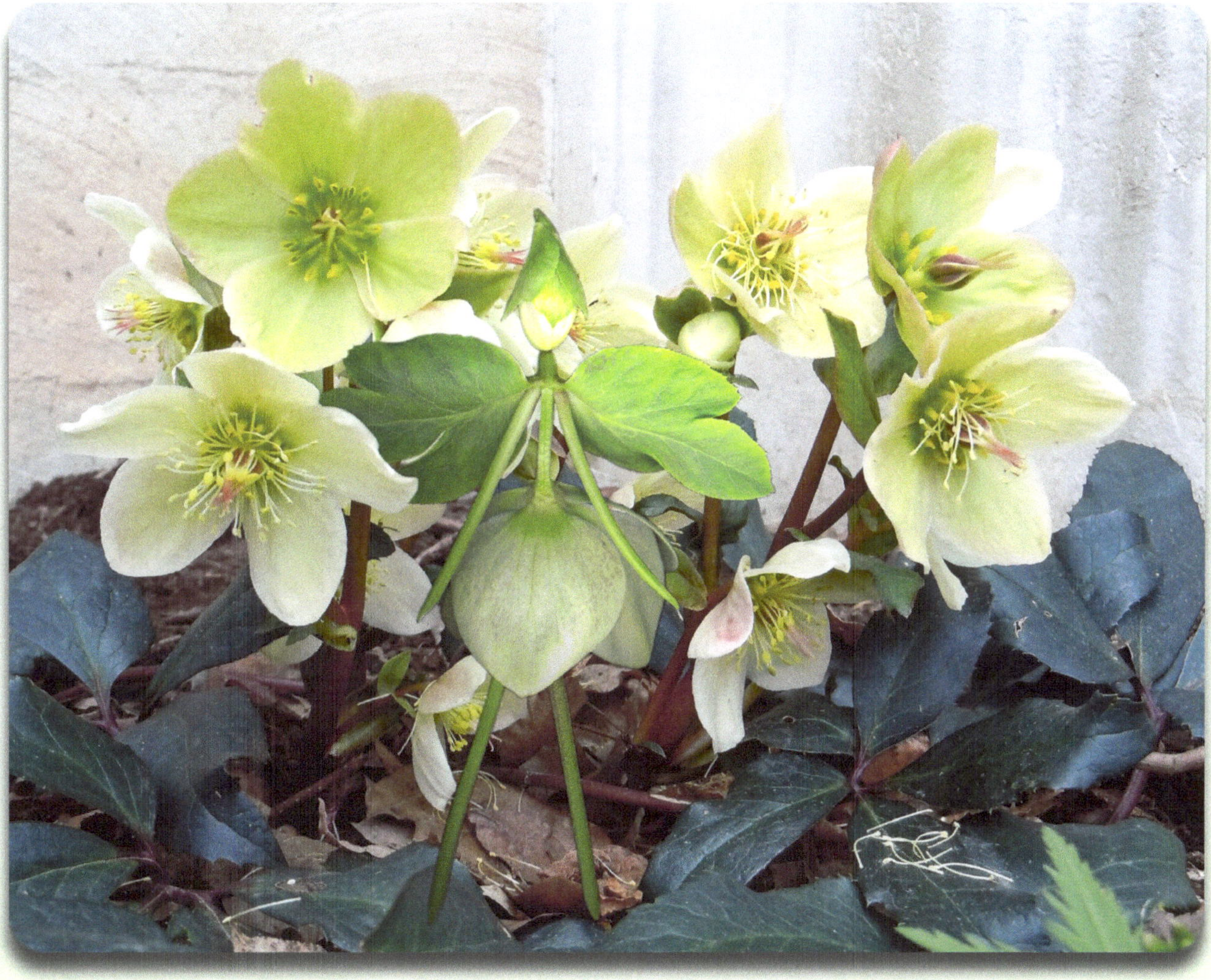

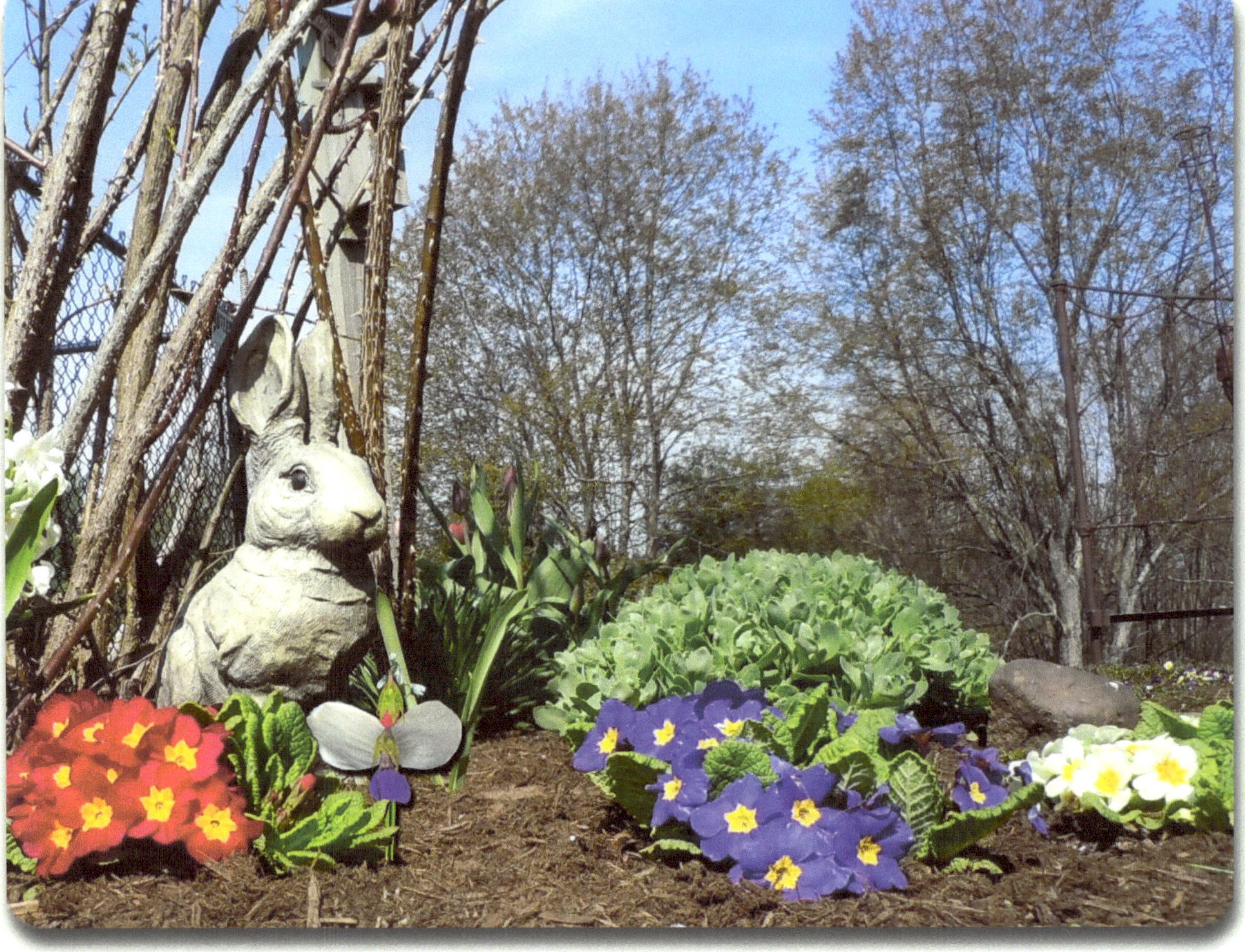

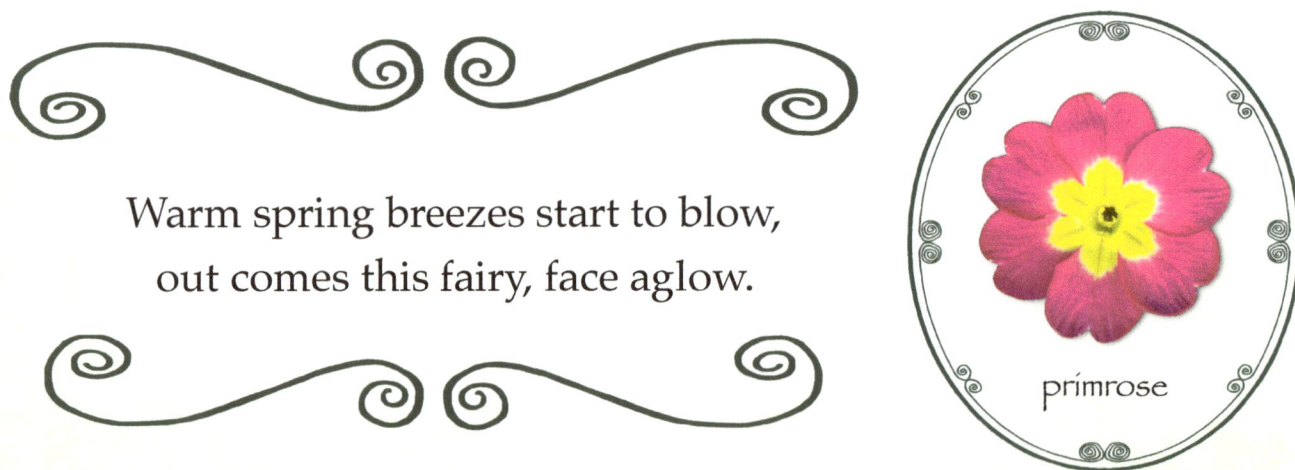

Warm spring breezes start to blow,
out comes this fairy, face aglow.

primrose

This season always brings rebirth
springing up from Mother Earth.

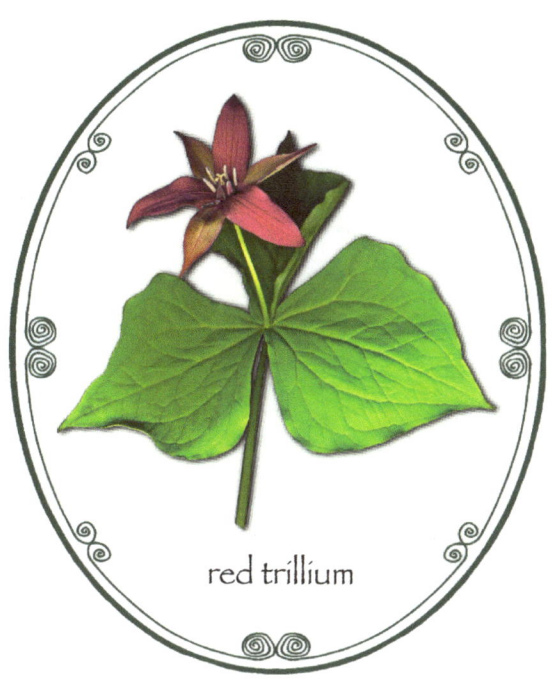

red trillium

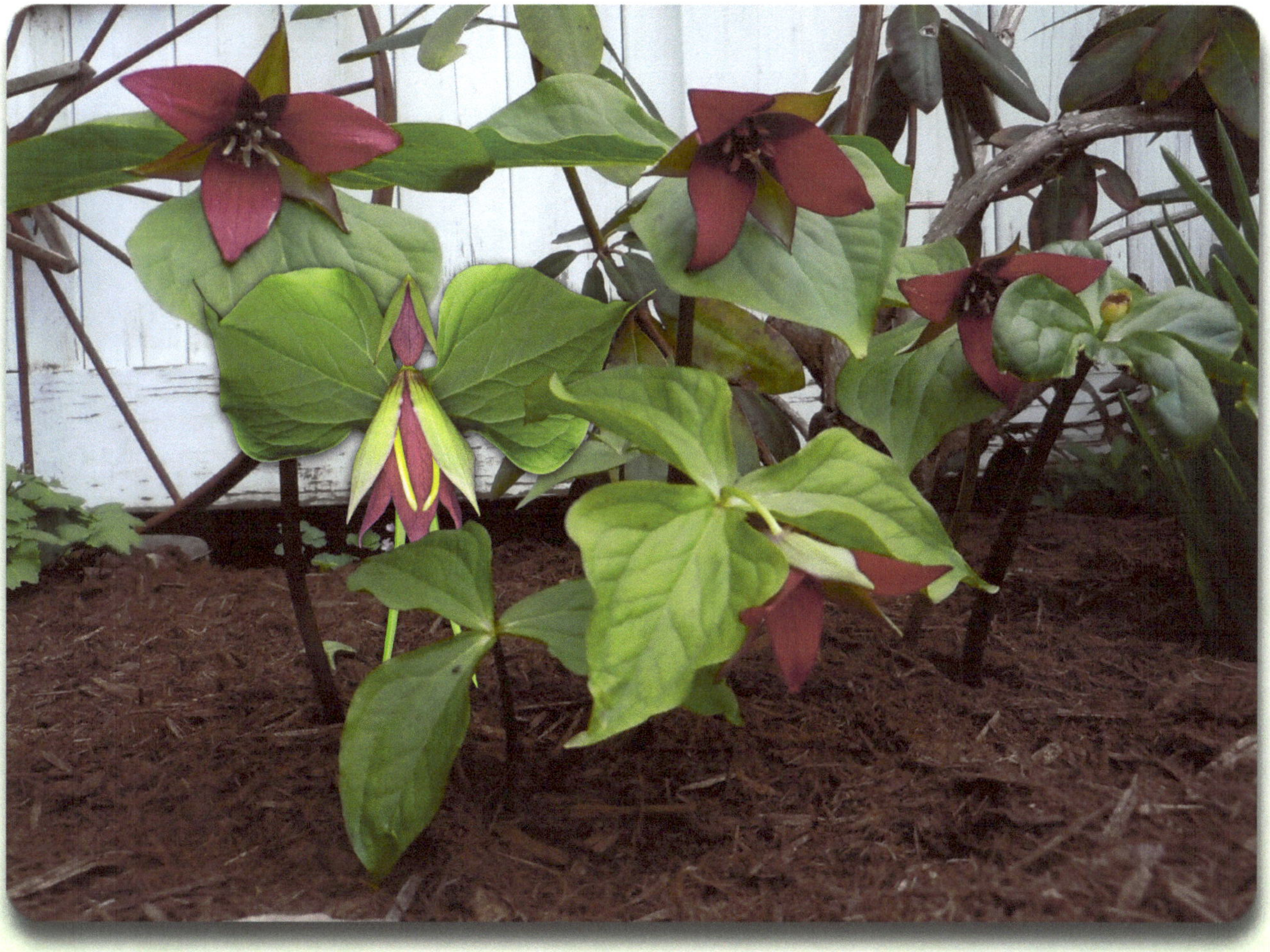

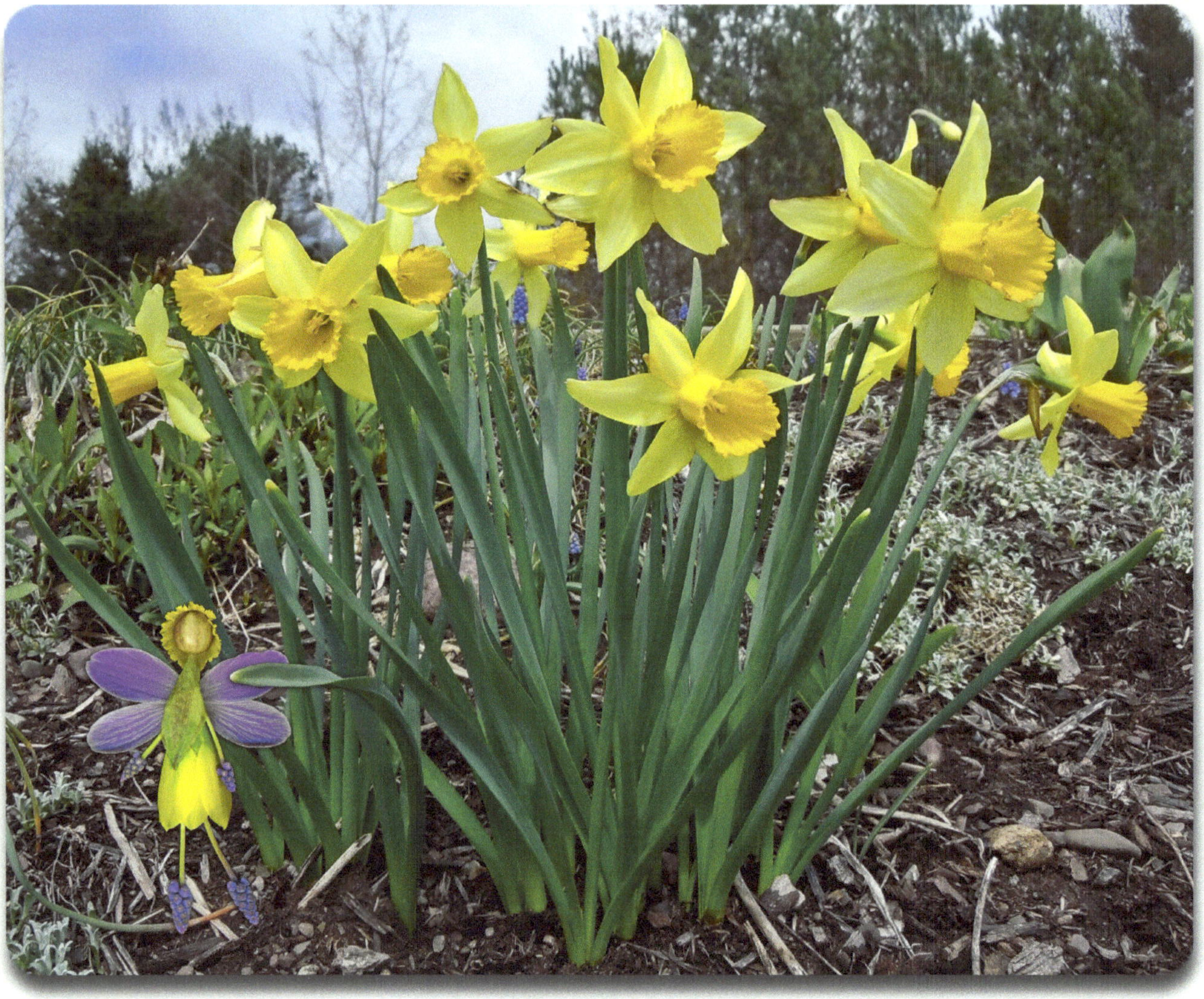

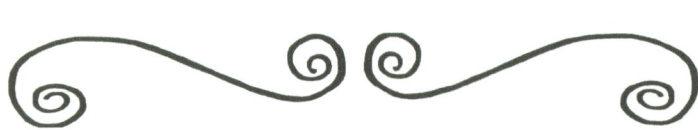

Daffodils glow bright and cheery.
lighting up what's dull or dreary.

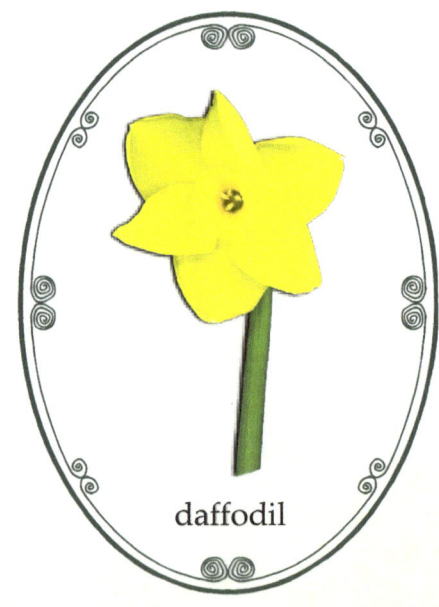

daffodil

She looks a bit like Little Bo Peep,
but tends wee fairies instead of sheep.

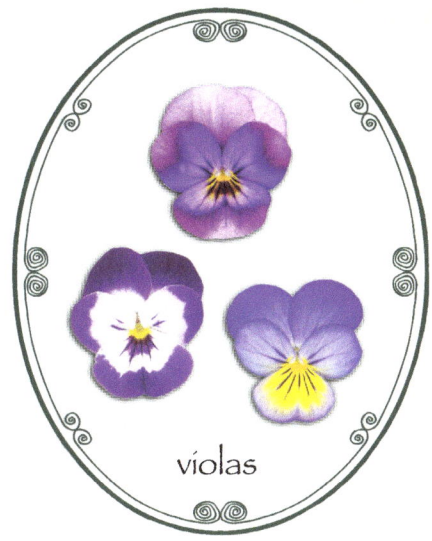

violas

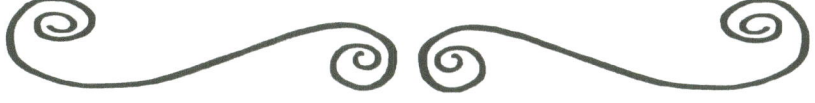

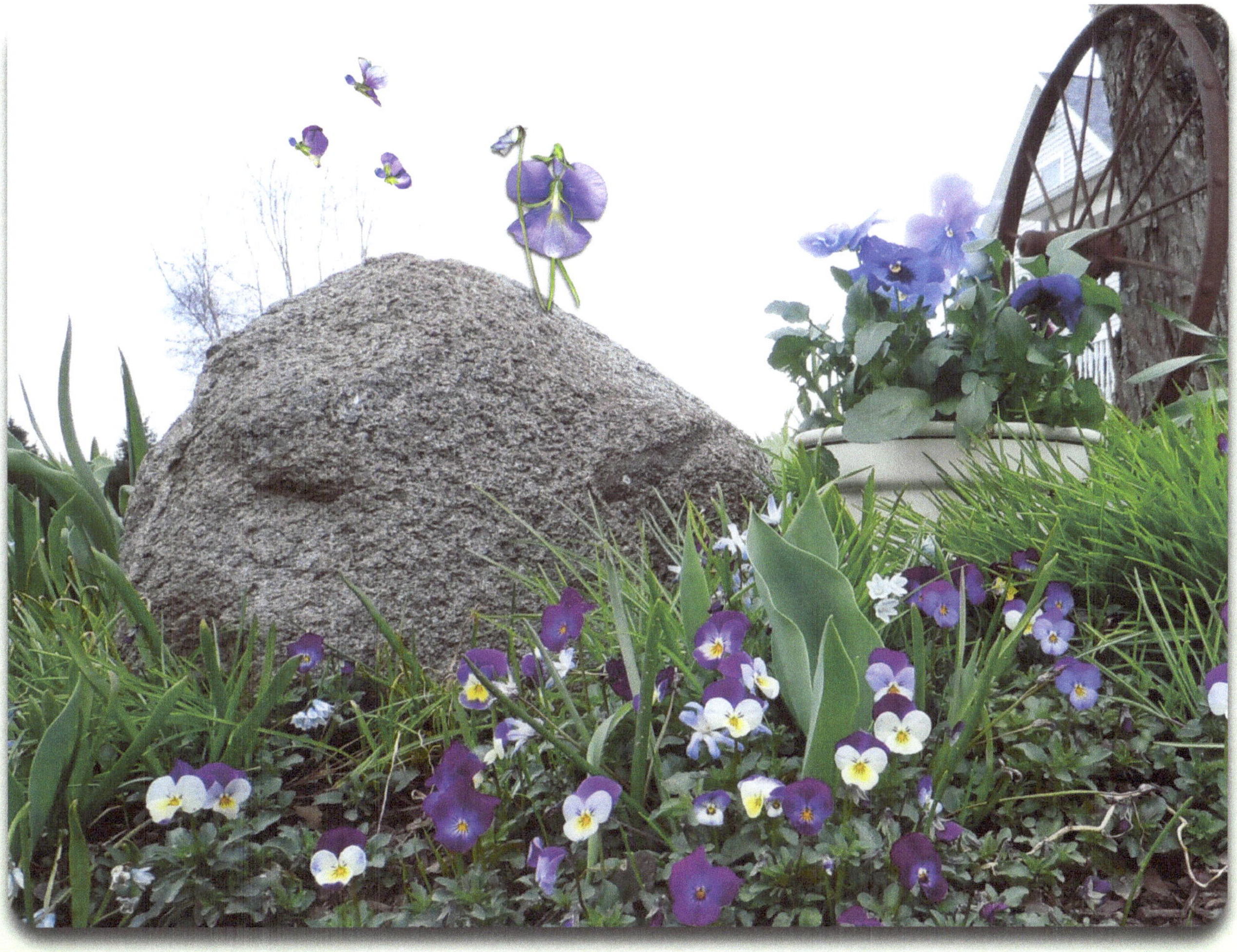

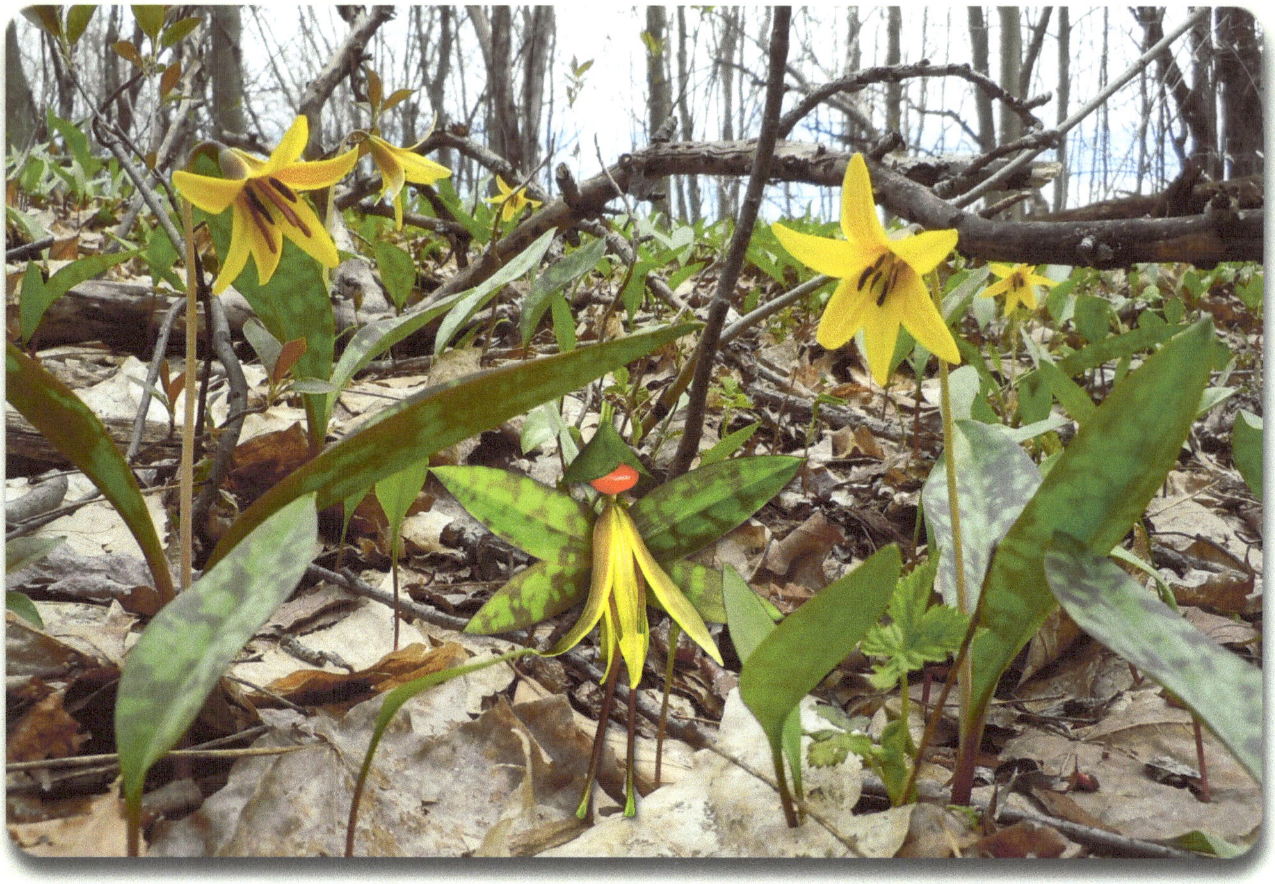

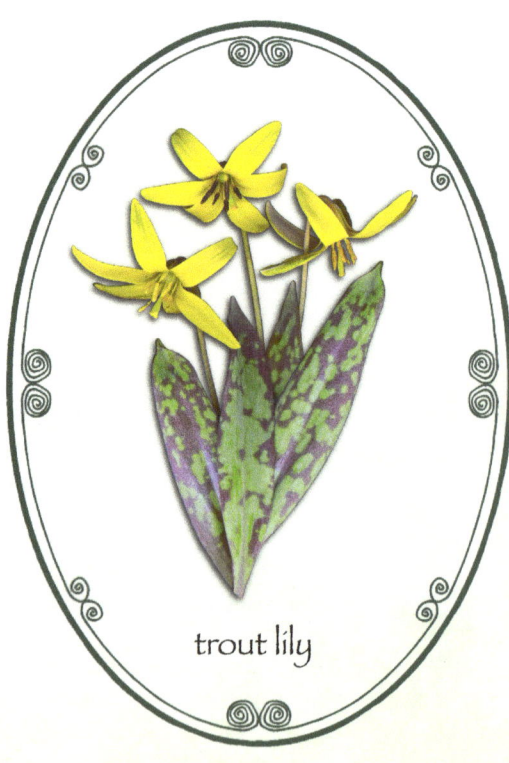

Look closely at a forest floor.
There's much to see. Let's explore!

trout lily

This purple fairy stopped to pose,
showing off her wings and clothes.

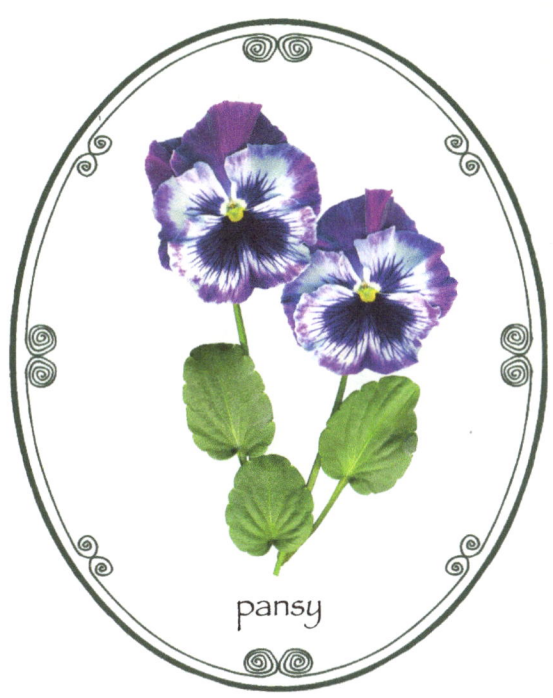

pansy

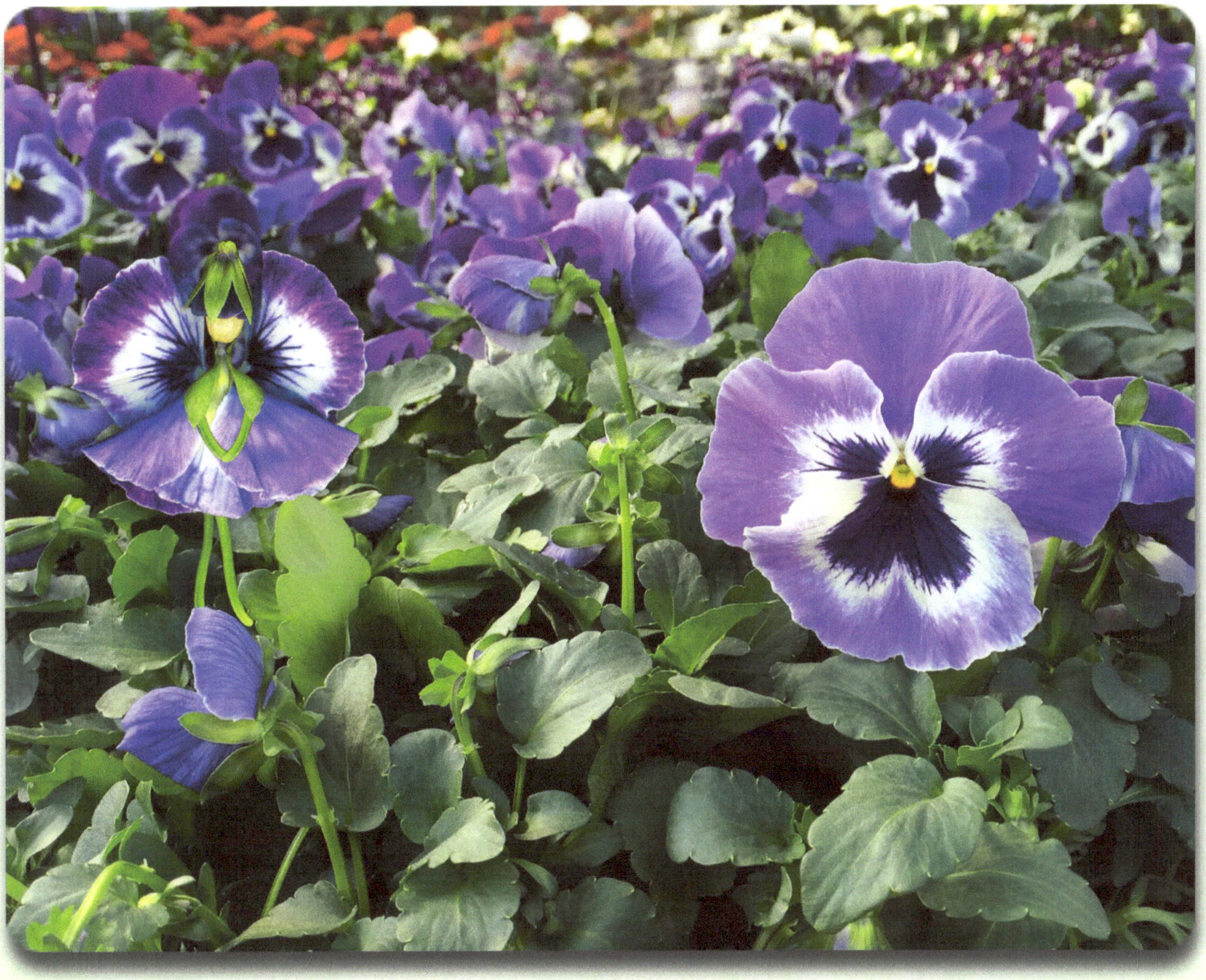

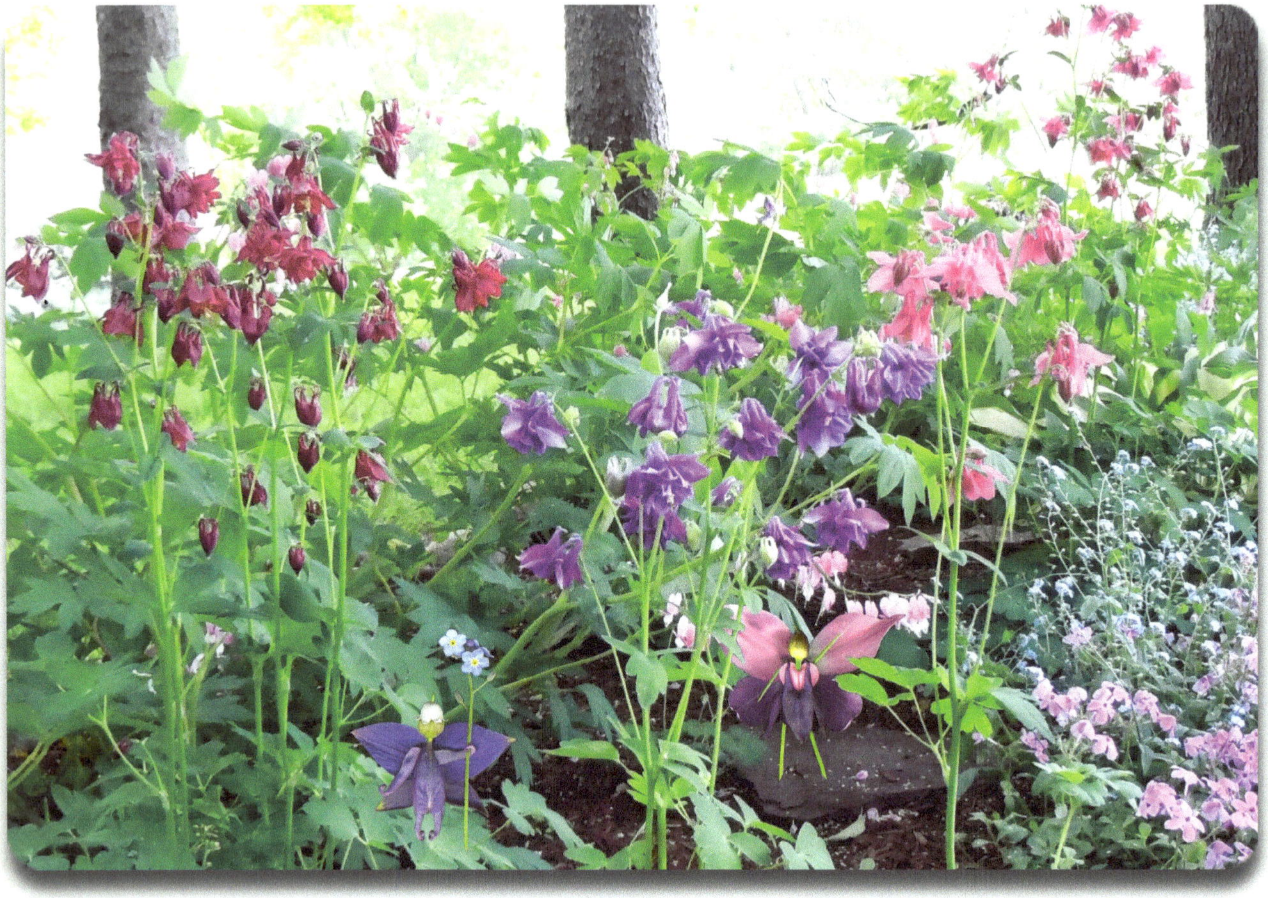

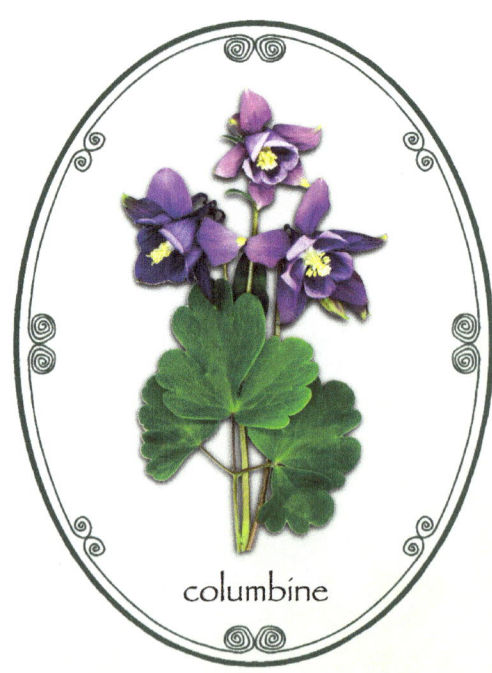

Two have fun with long-stalked flowers,
playing hide-and-seek for hours.

columbine

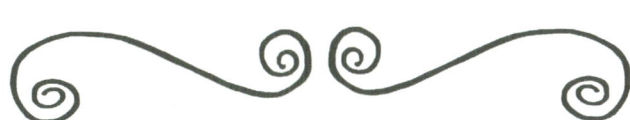

Fairy sisters, so carefree,
grace this starry flowered tree.

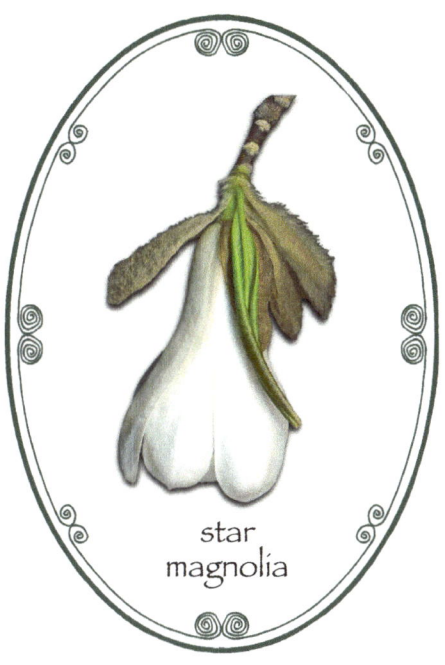

star
magnolia

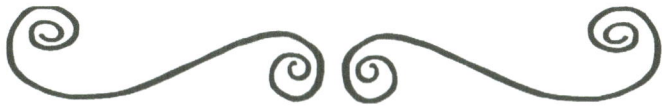

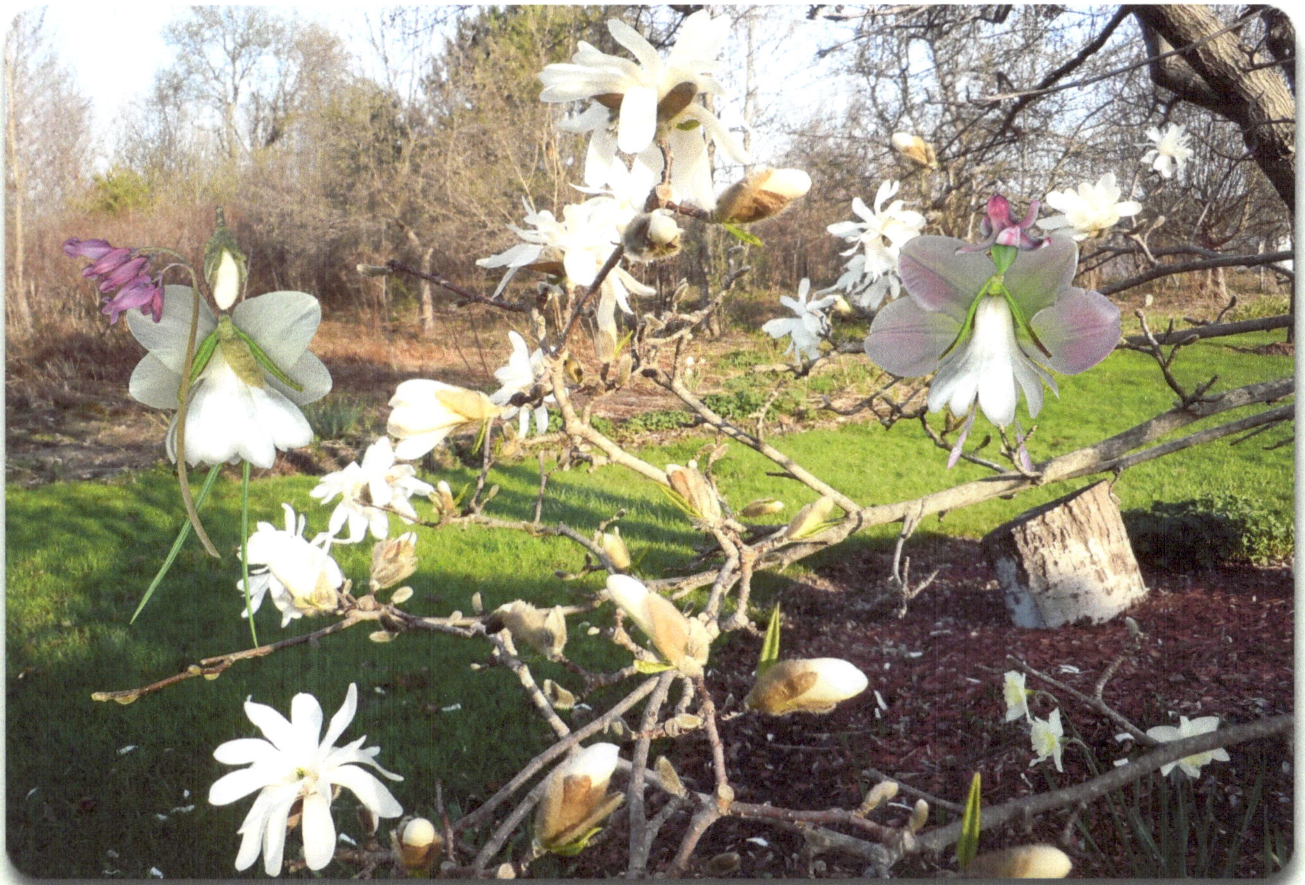

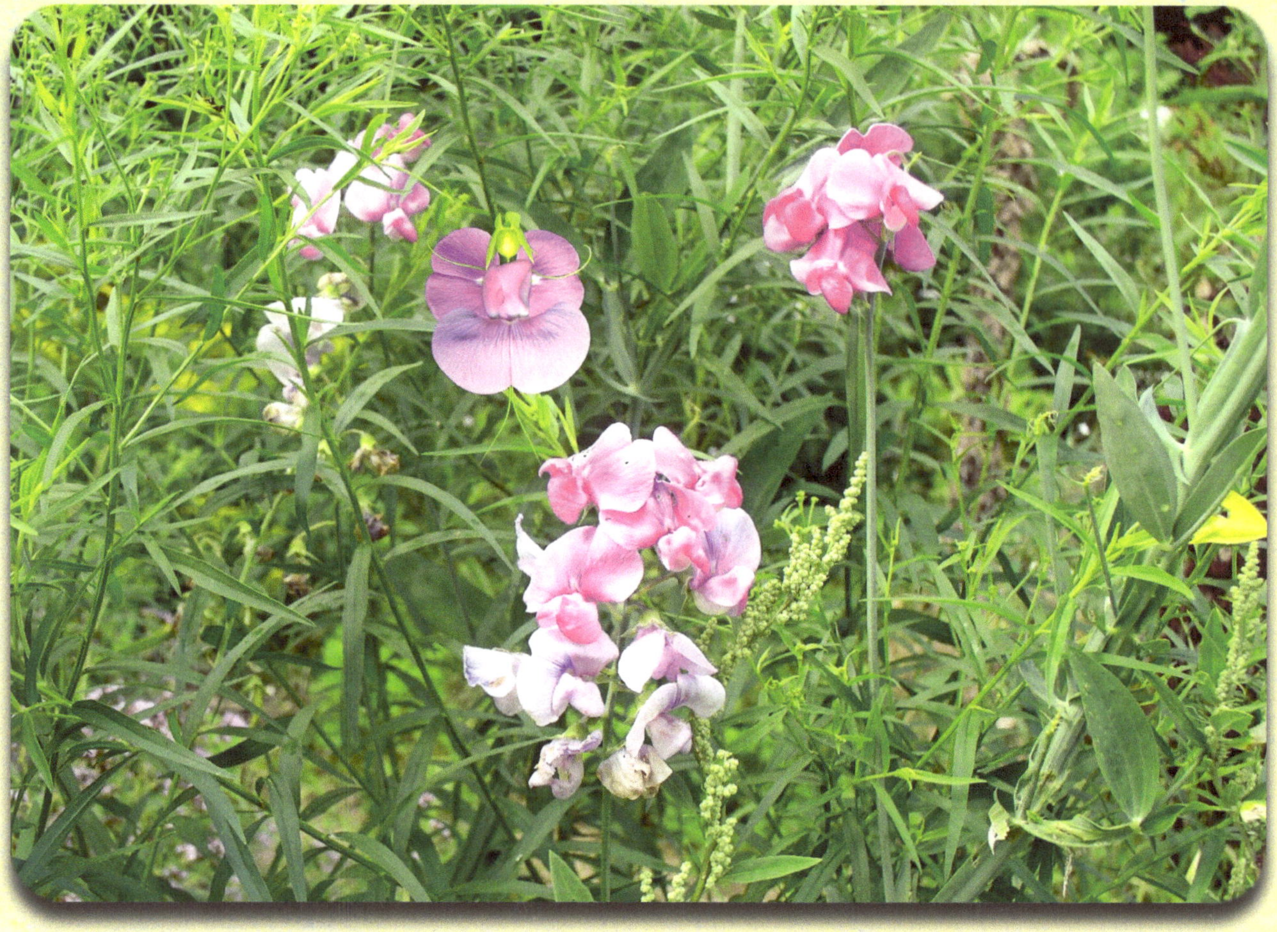

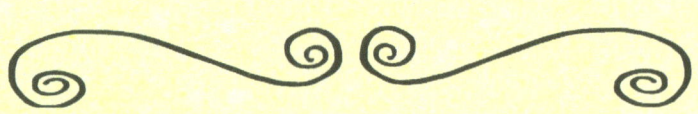

Wild peas with blooms so sweet,
open up in summer's heat.

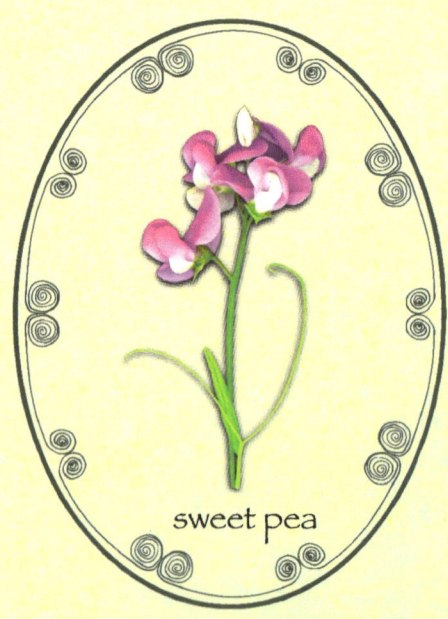

sweet pea

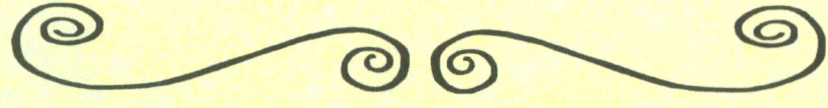

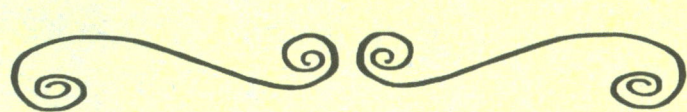

A cheerful fairy loves this bloom
with spikes of red and spiced perfume.

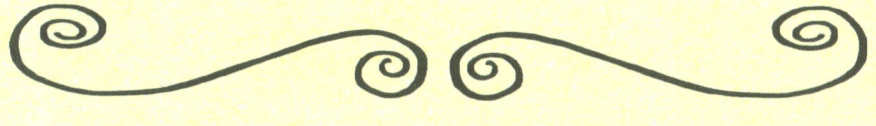

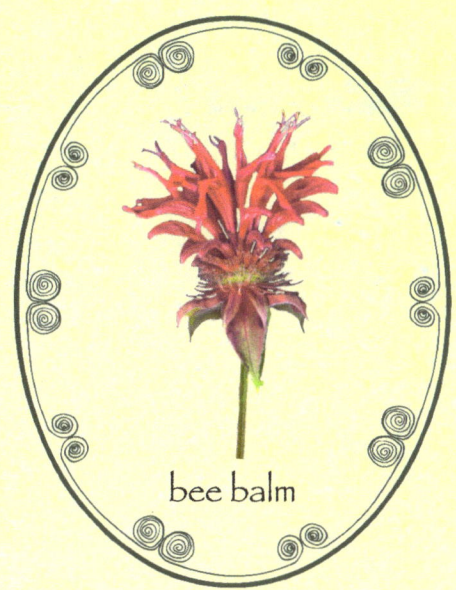

bee balm

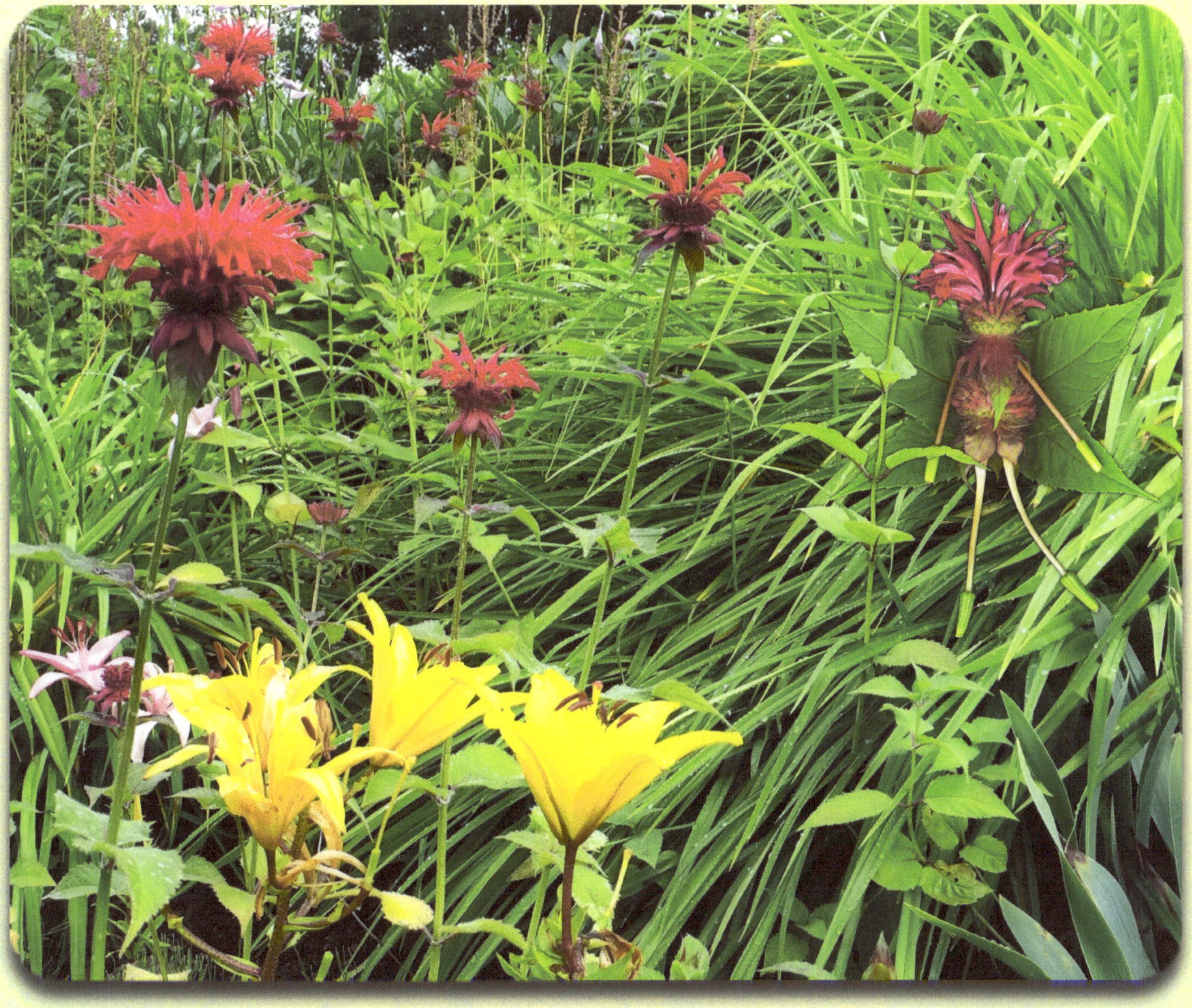

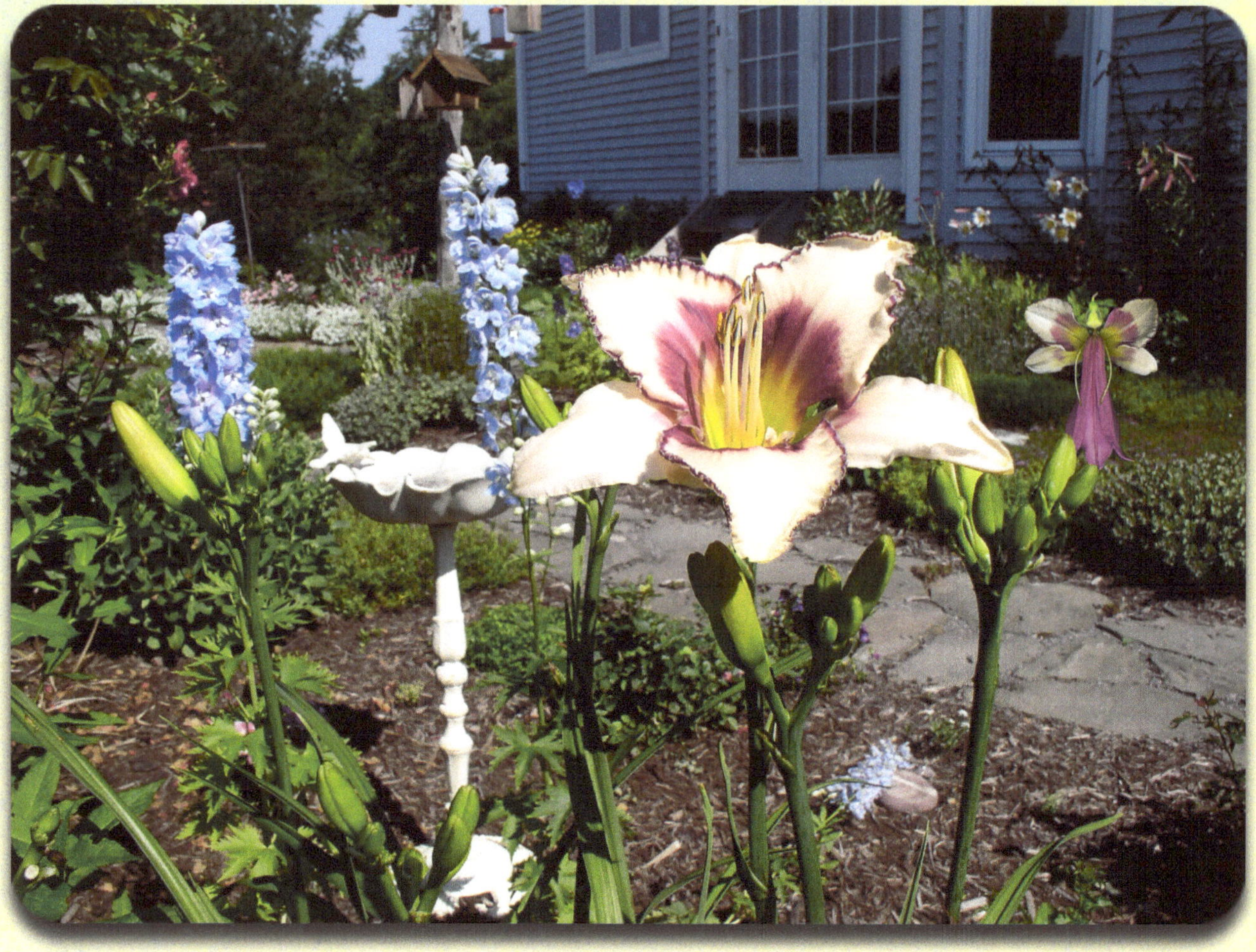

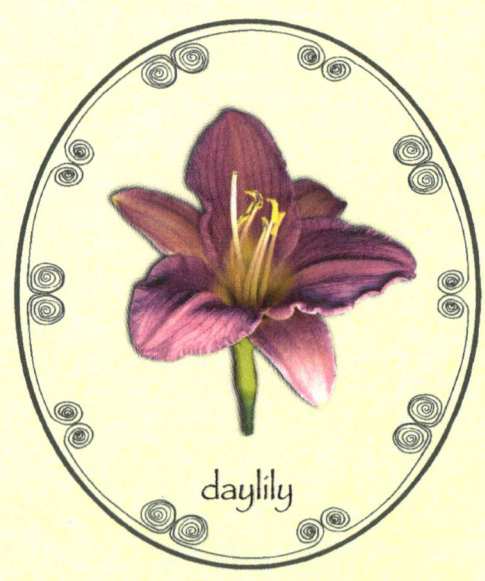

She loves warmer, lazy days,
enjoying summer's stronger rays.

daylily

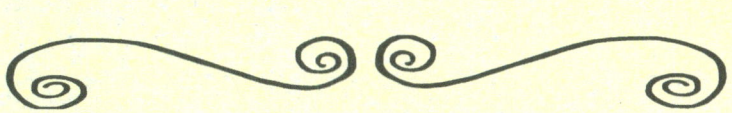

He swoops about, bold and free,
like a busy bumblebee.

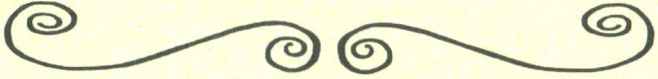

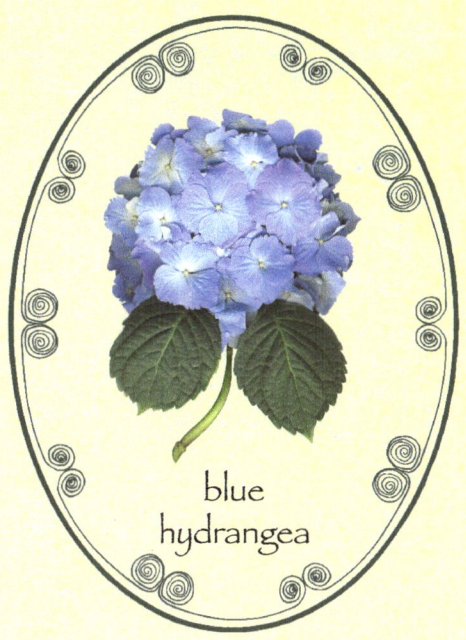

blue
hydrangea

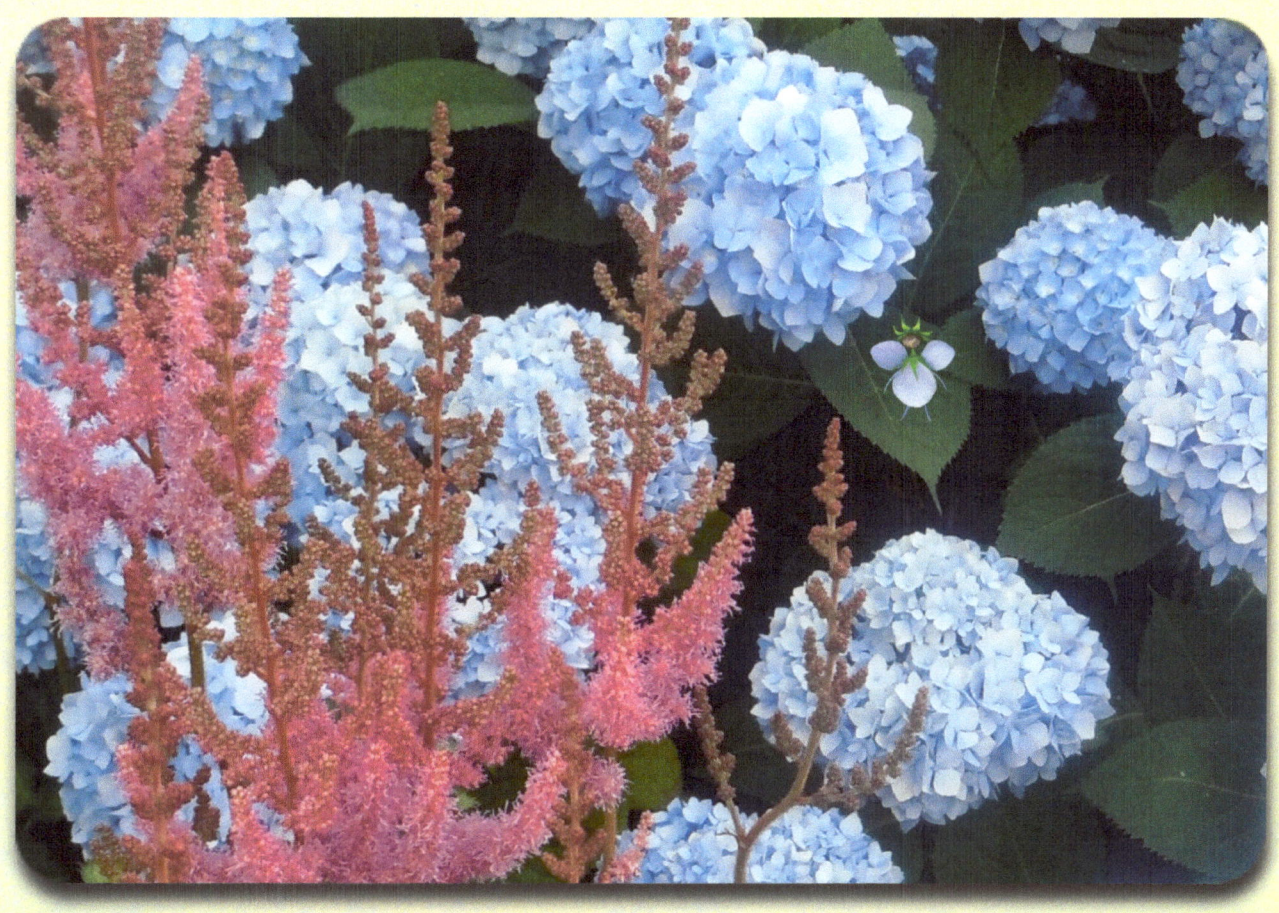

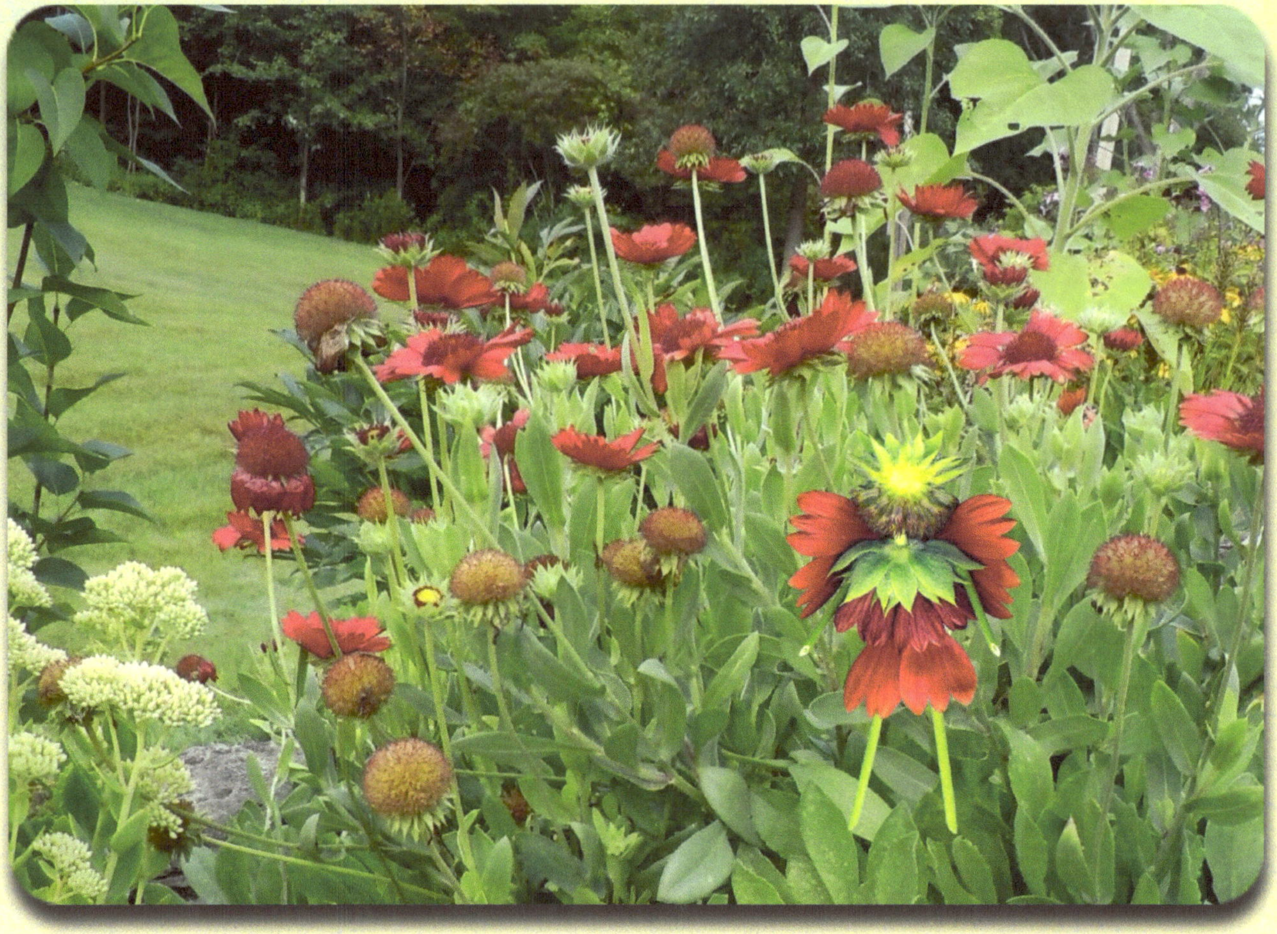

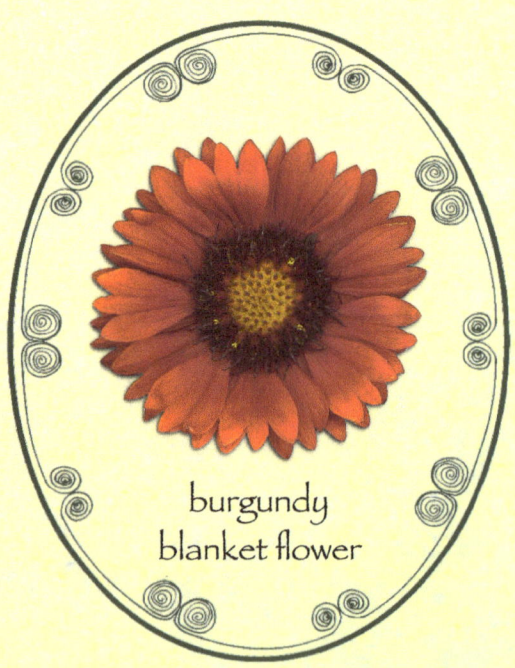

Fairy and flowers, bold and red,
rule this summer flowerbed.

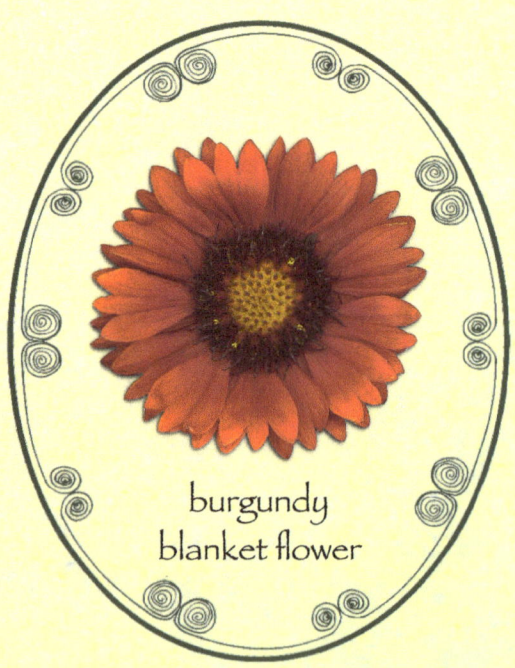

burgundy
blanket flower

The buds expand, big and round,
bursting wide without a sound!

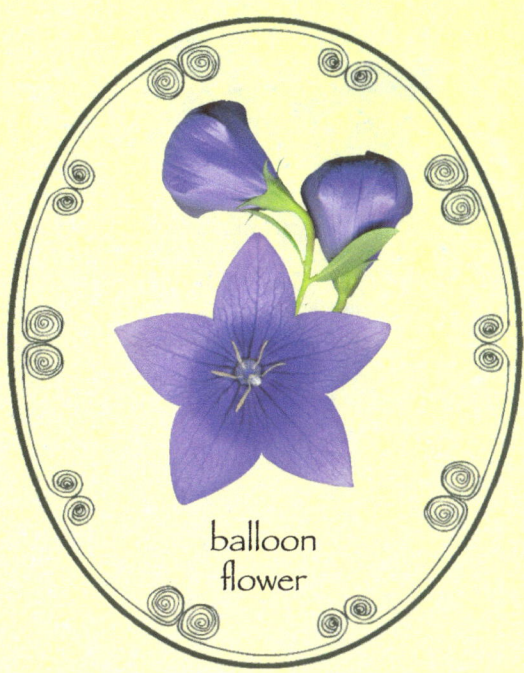

balloon
flower

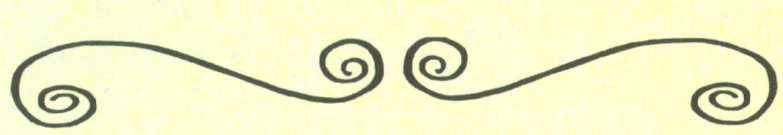

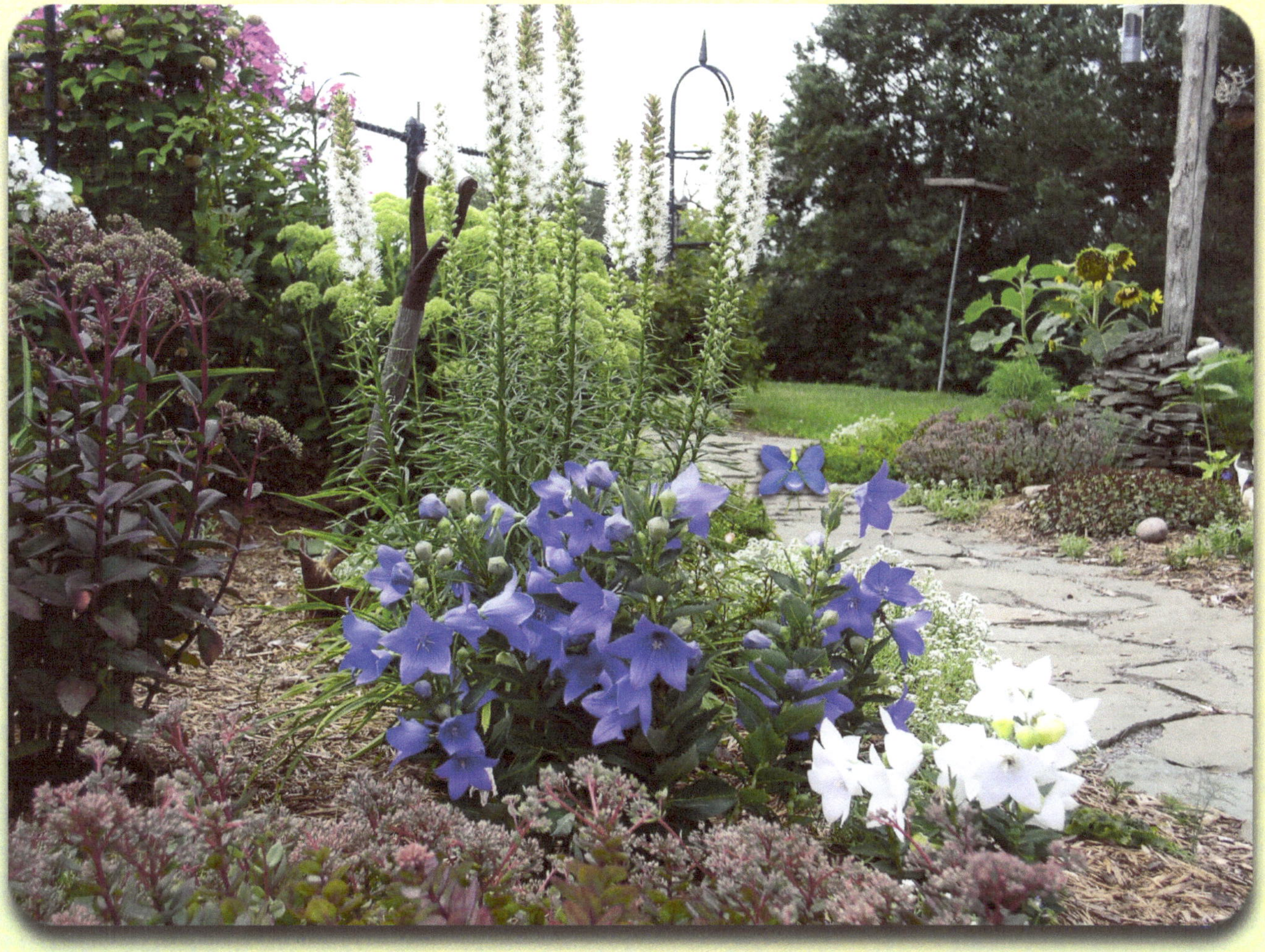

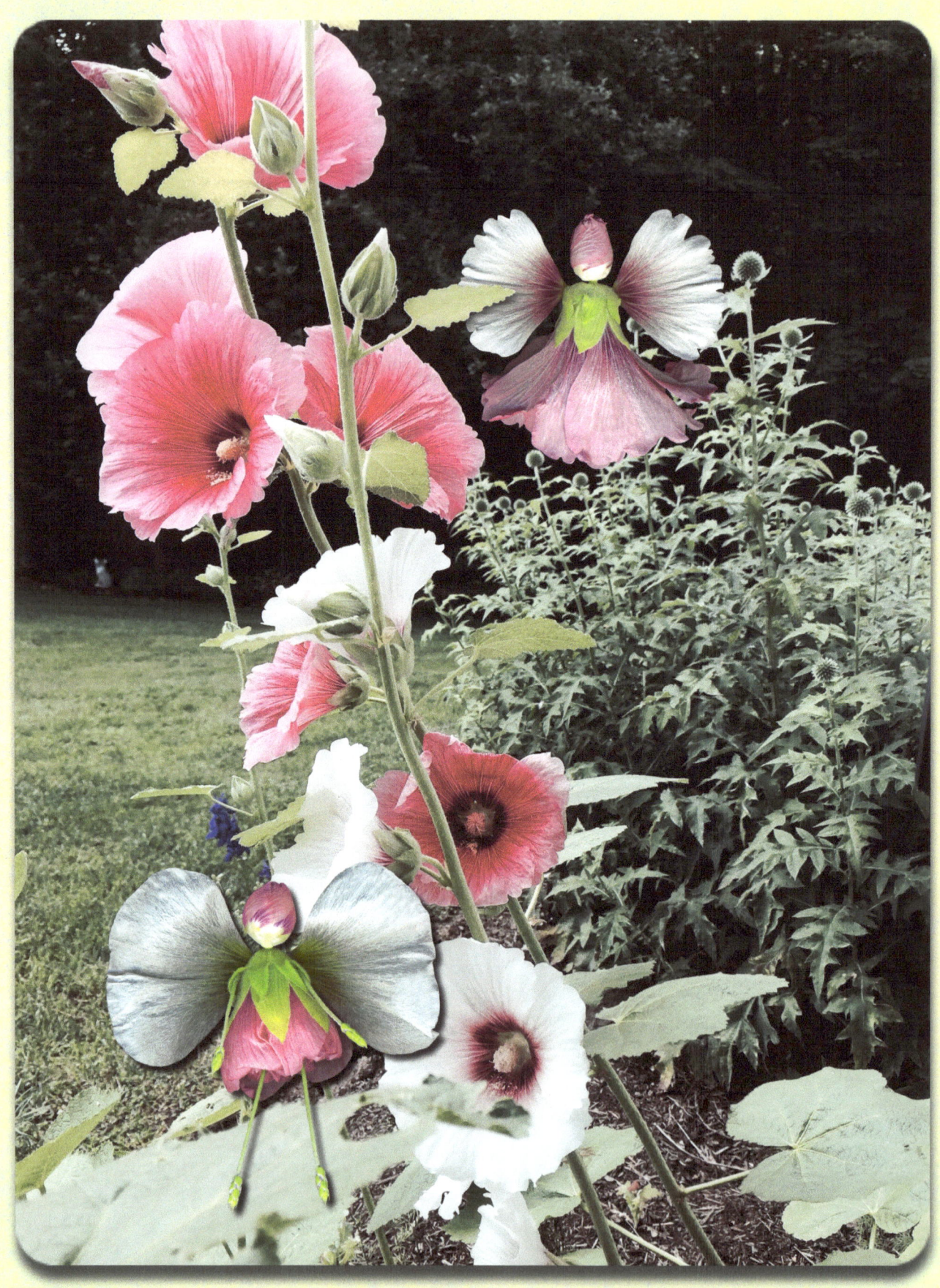

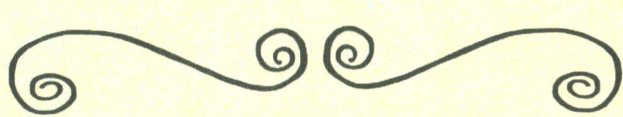

Bell-shaped flowers growing tall
make lovely gowns for three so small.

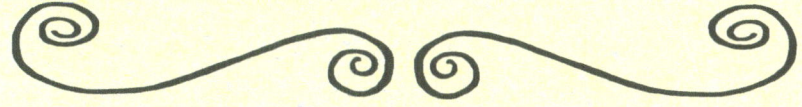

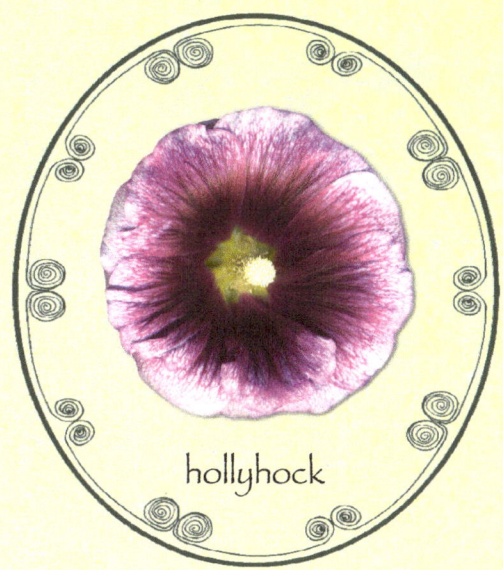

hollyhock

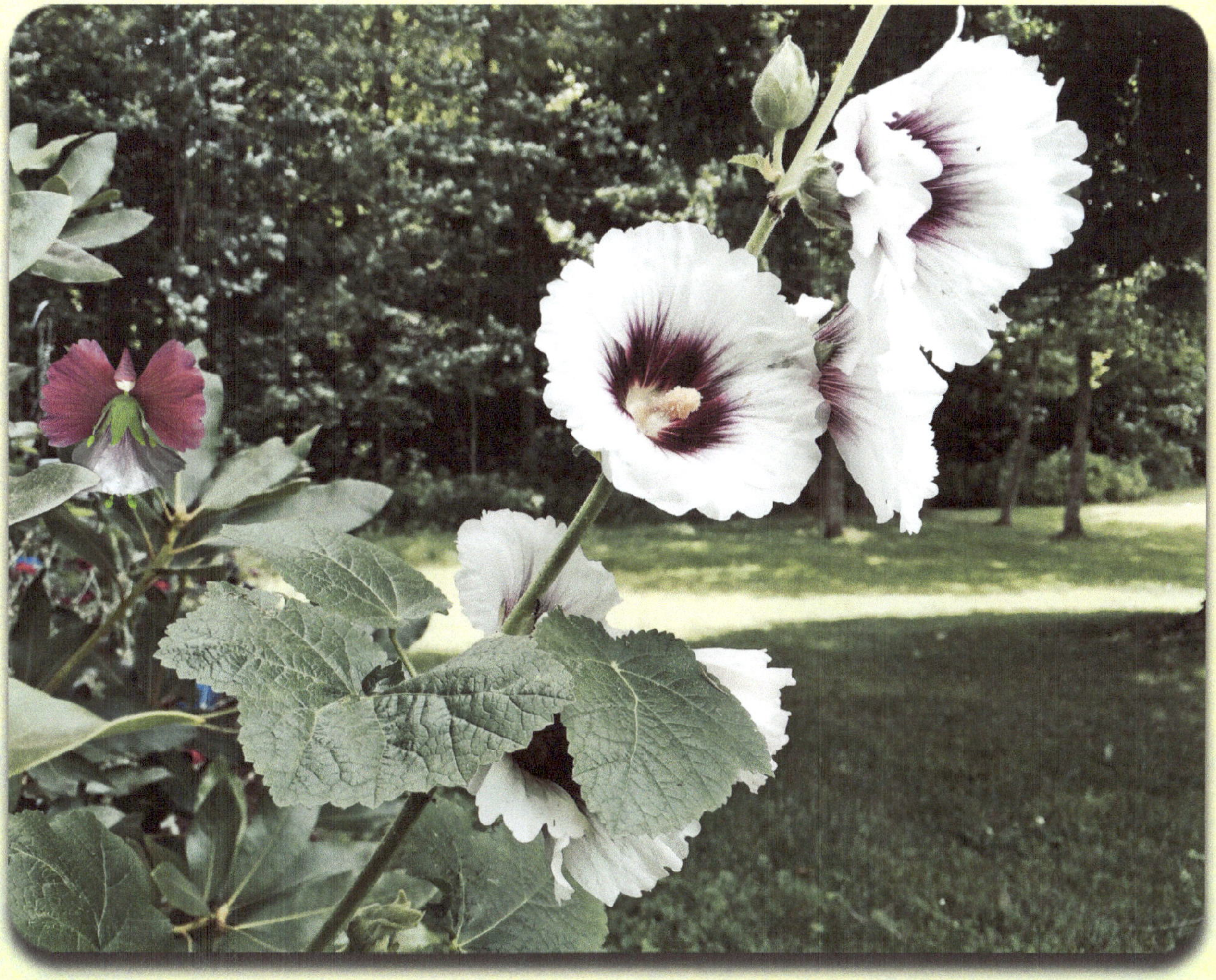

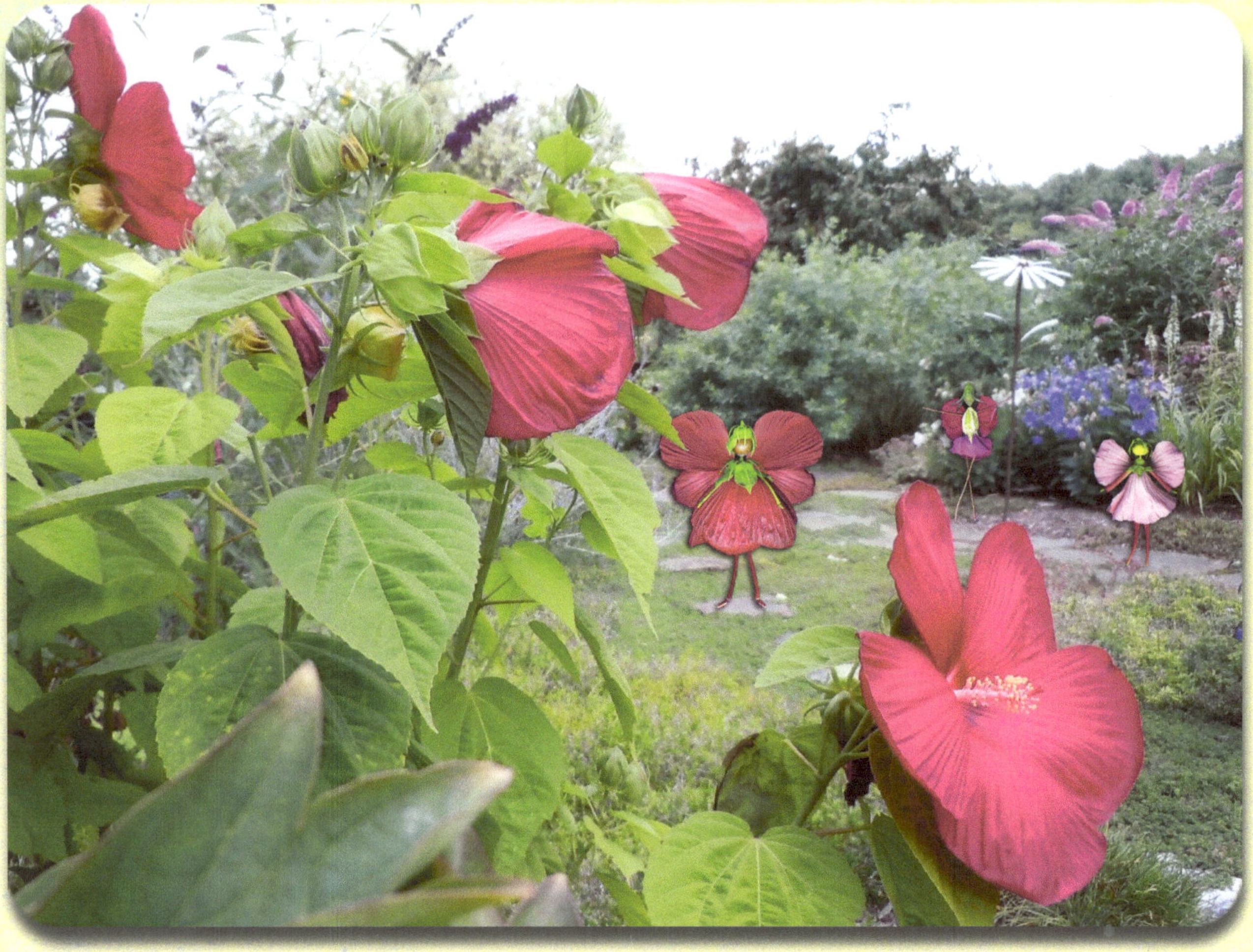

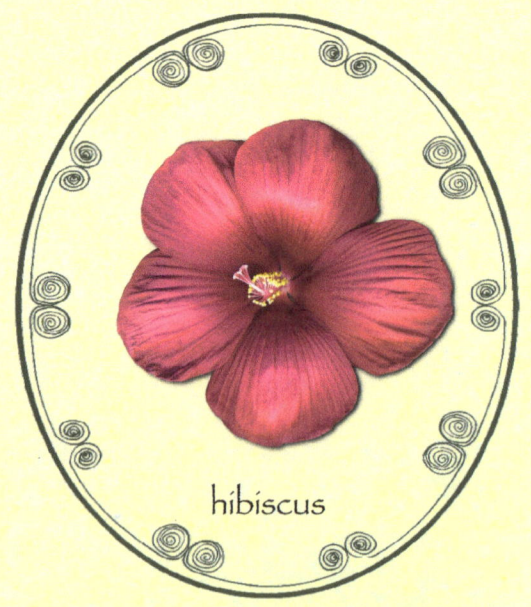

Summer friends enjoy the day,
they know it isn't here to stay.

hibiscus

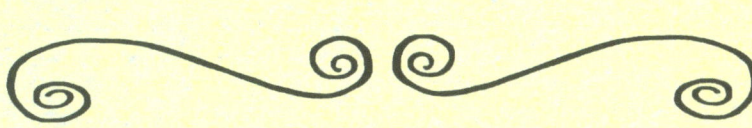

Blooms and fairies, shining bright,
mirror summer's fading light.

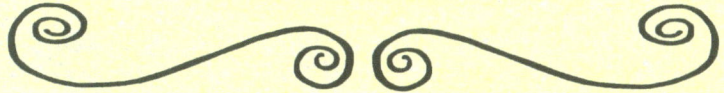

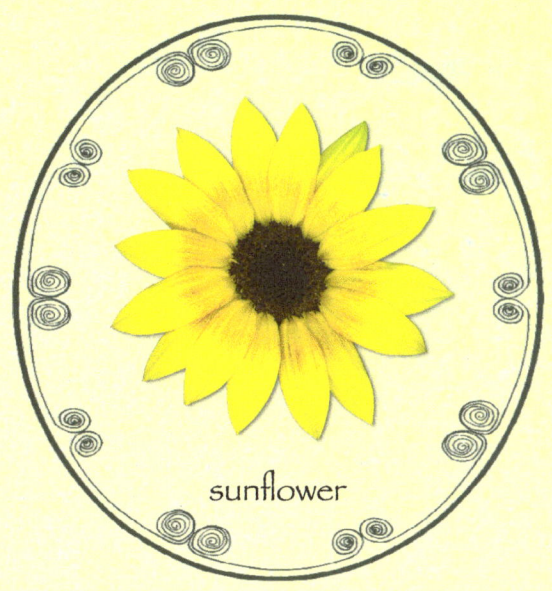

sunflower

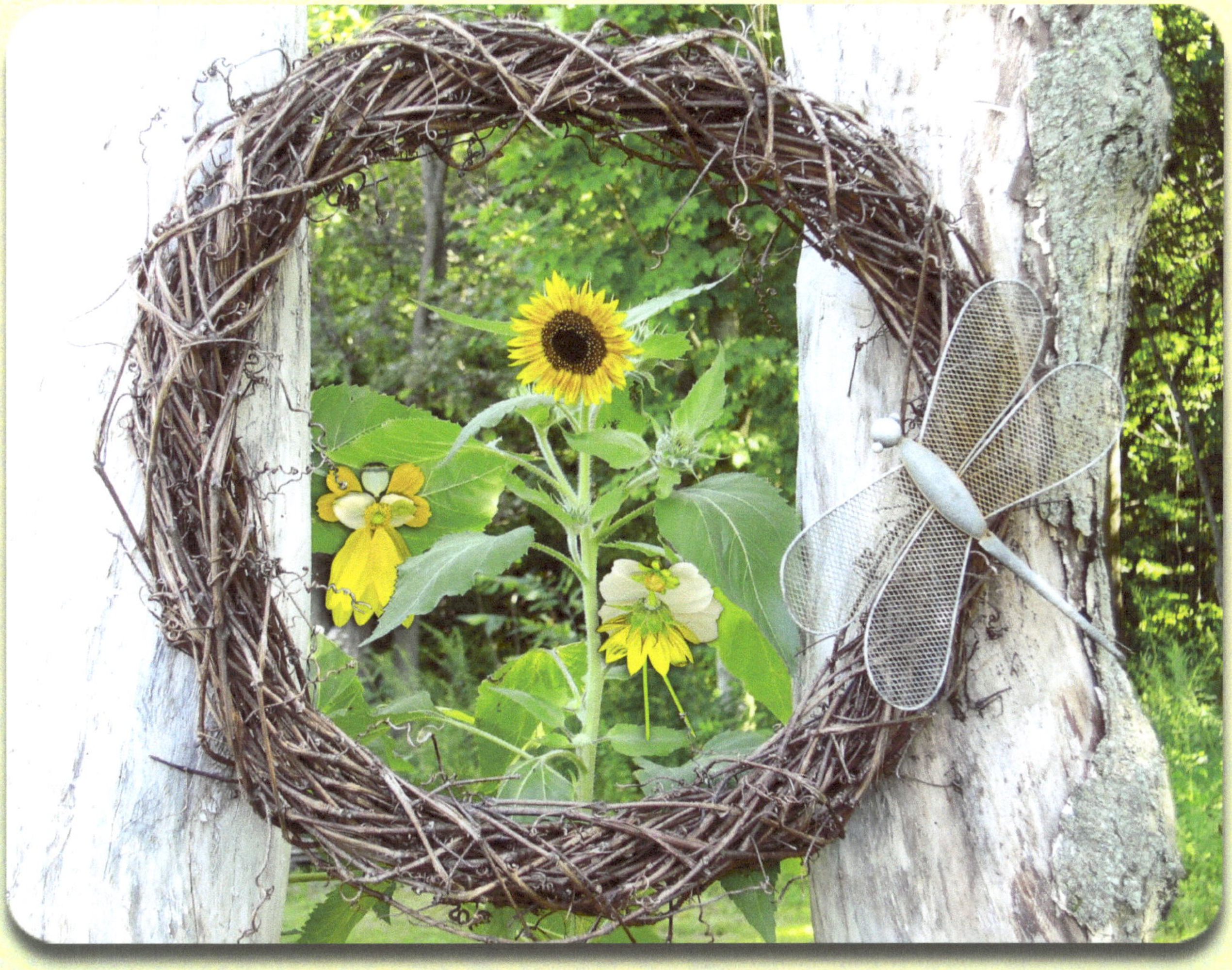

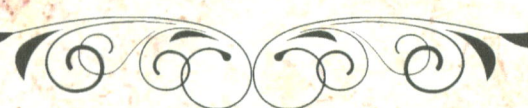

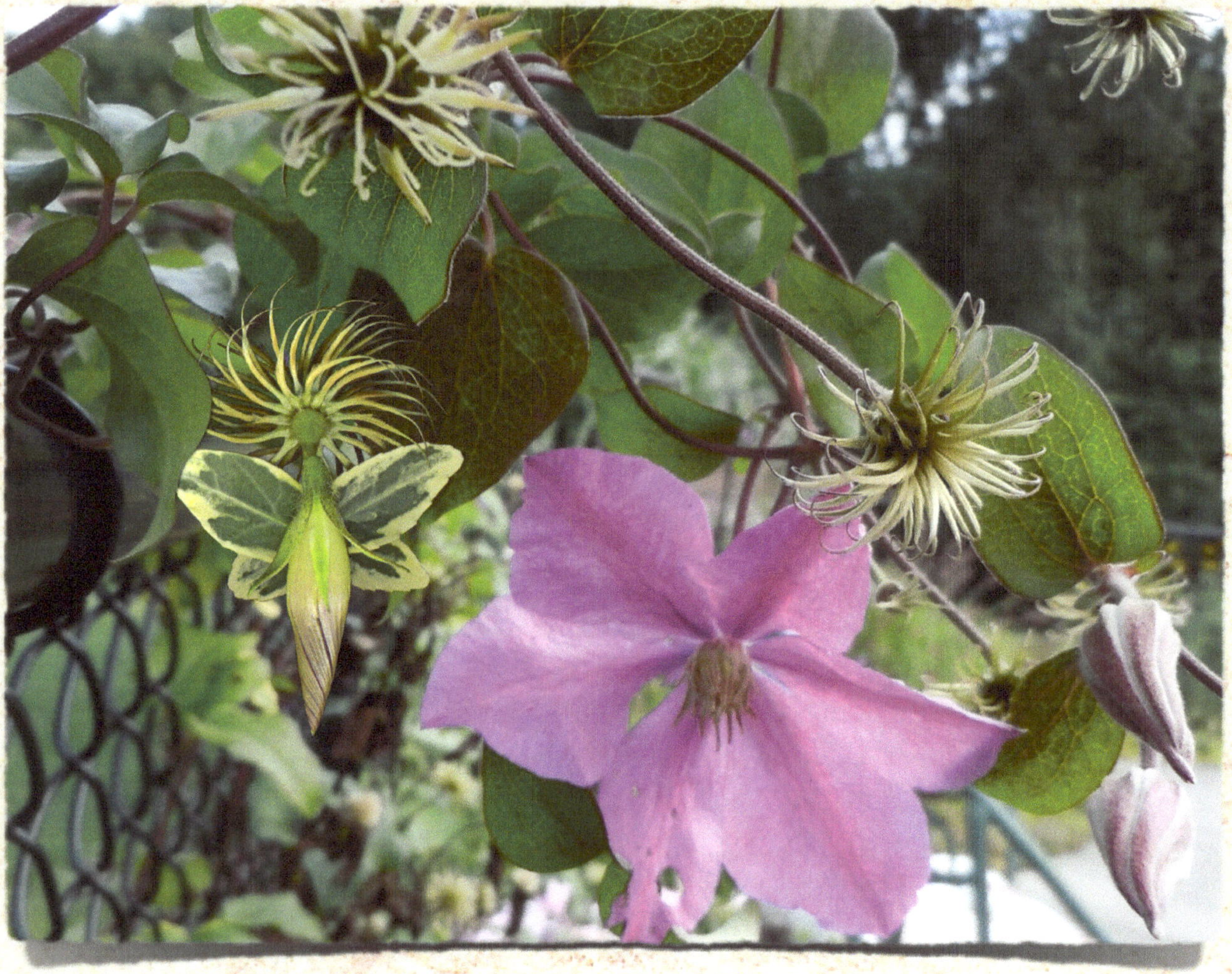

Plants form seeds this time of year,
different fairies now appear.

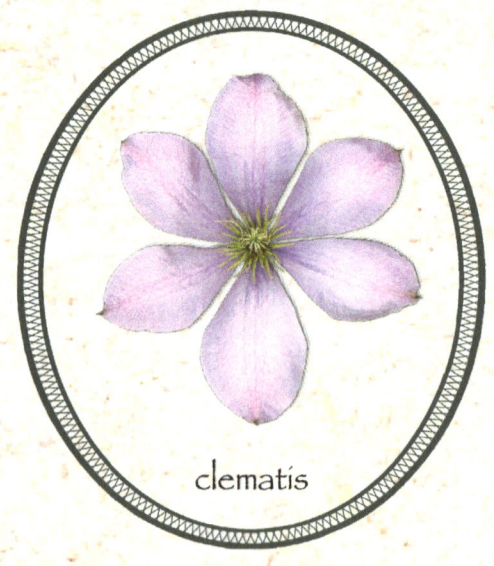

clematis

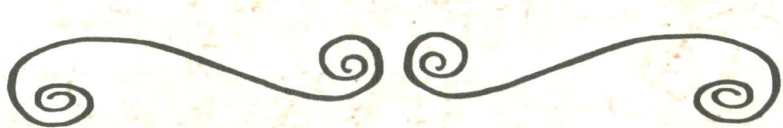

Days get short and cool winds blow,
leaves and wings begin to glow.

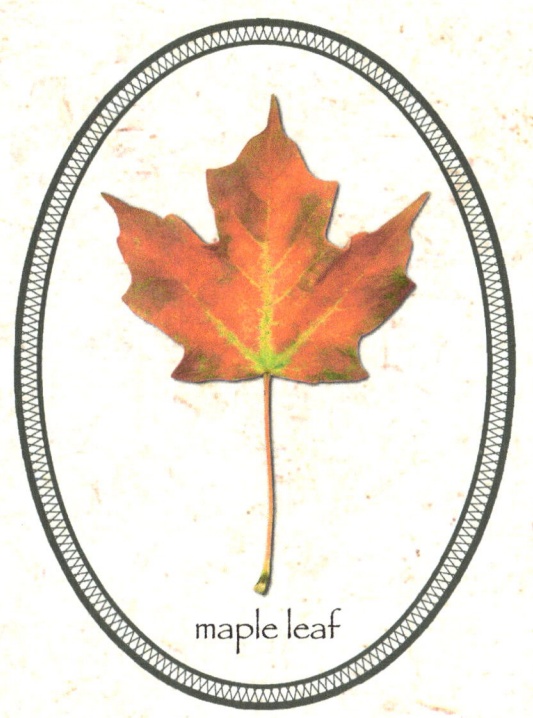

maple leaf

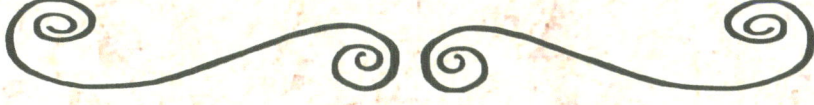

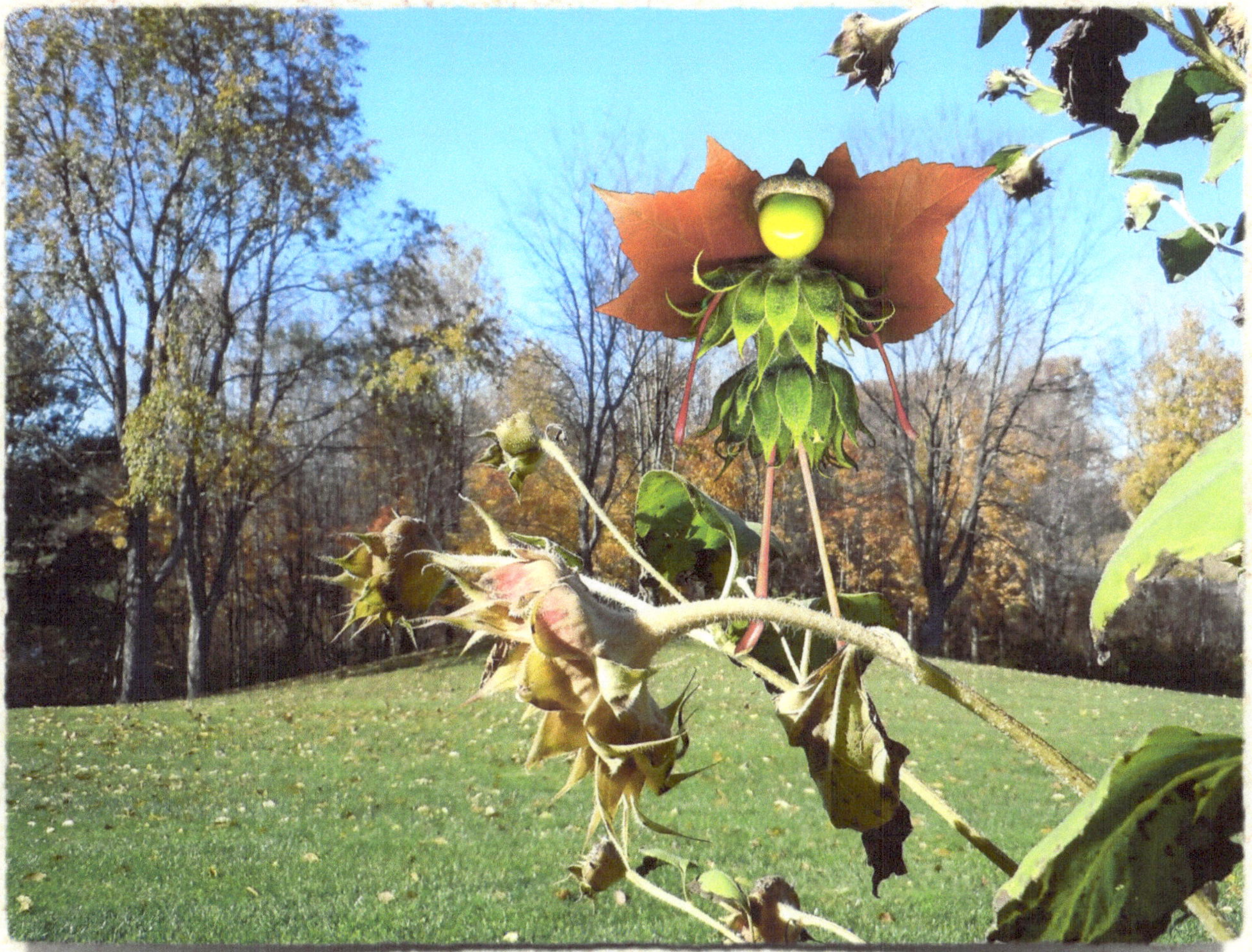

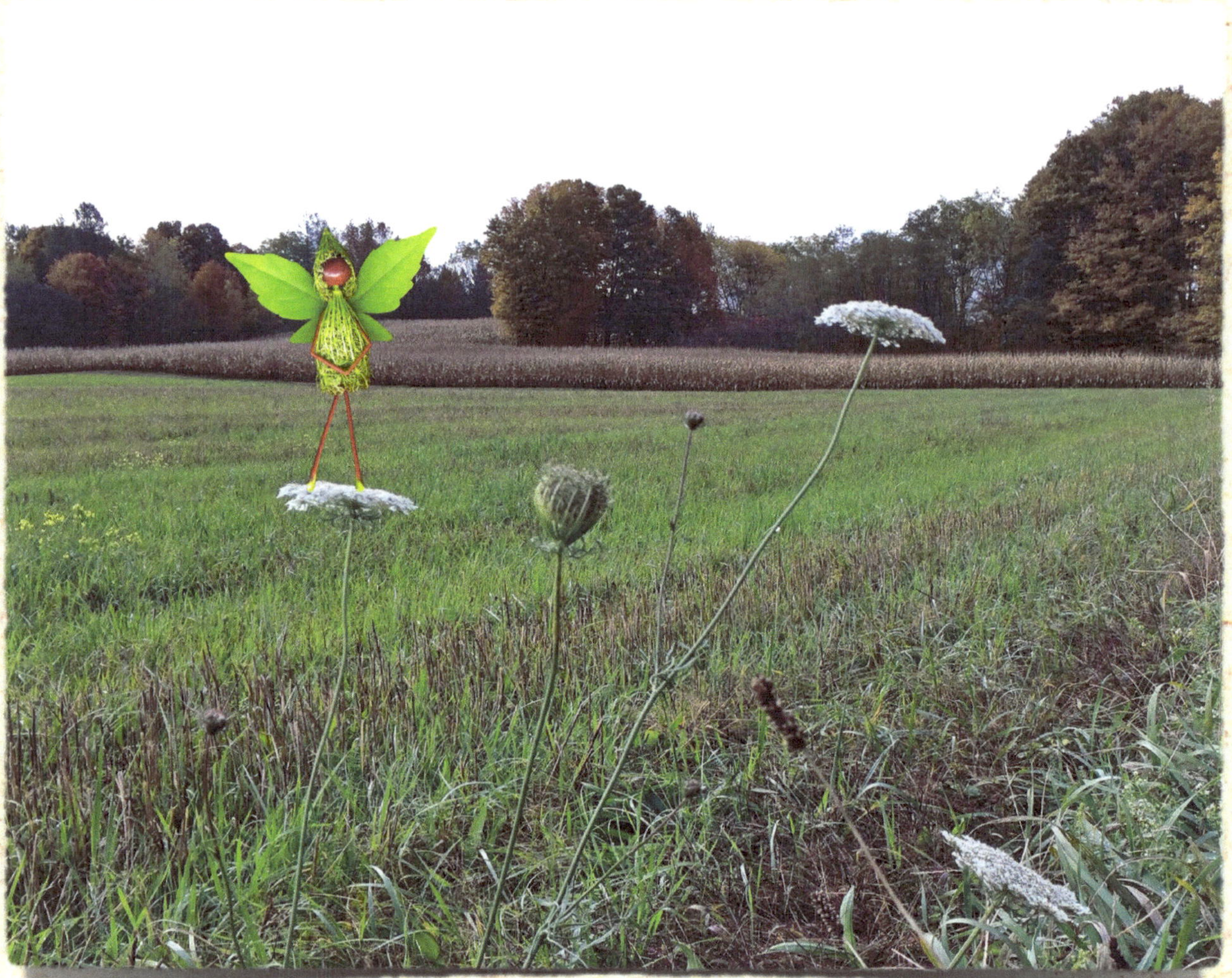

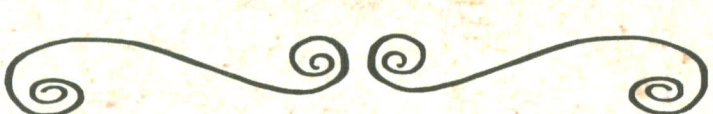

Even with gray skies around,
there's some brightness to be found.

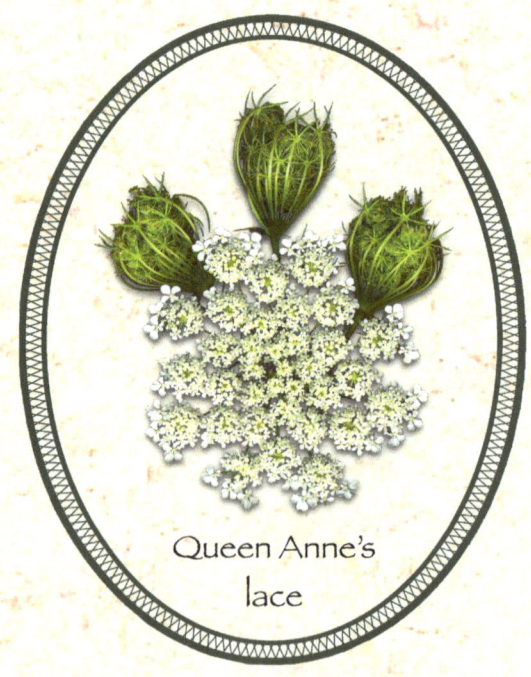

Queen Anne's
lace

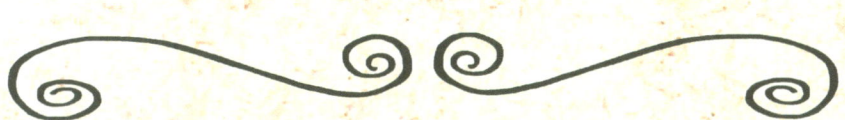

Nights grow cold and there's a freeze,
Mother Nature paints the trees.

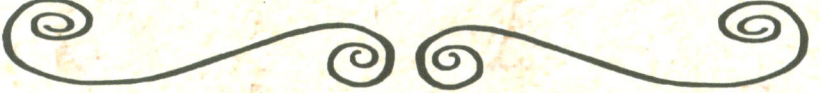

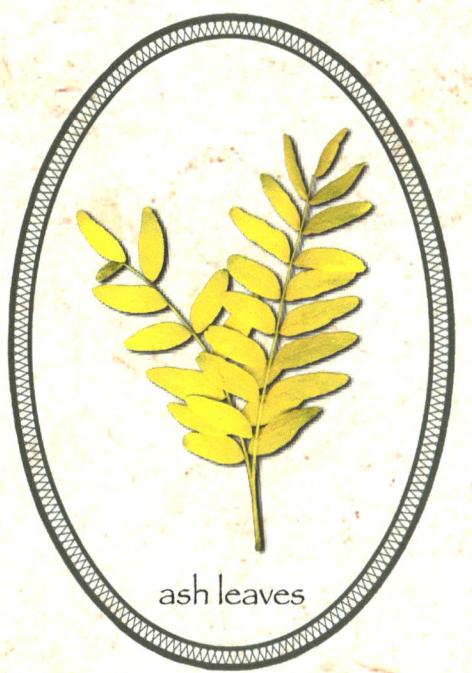

ash leaves

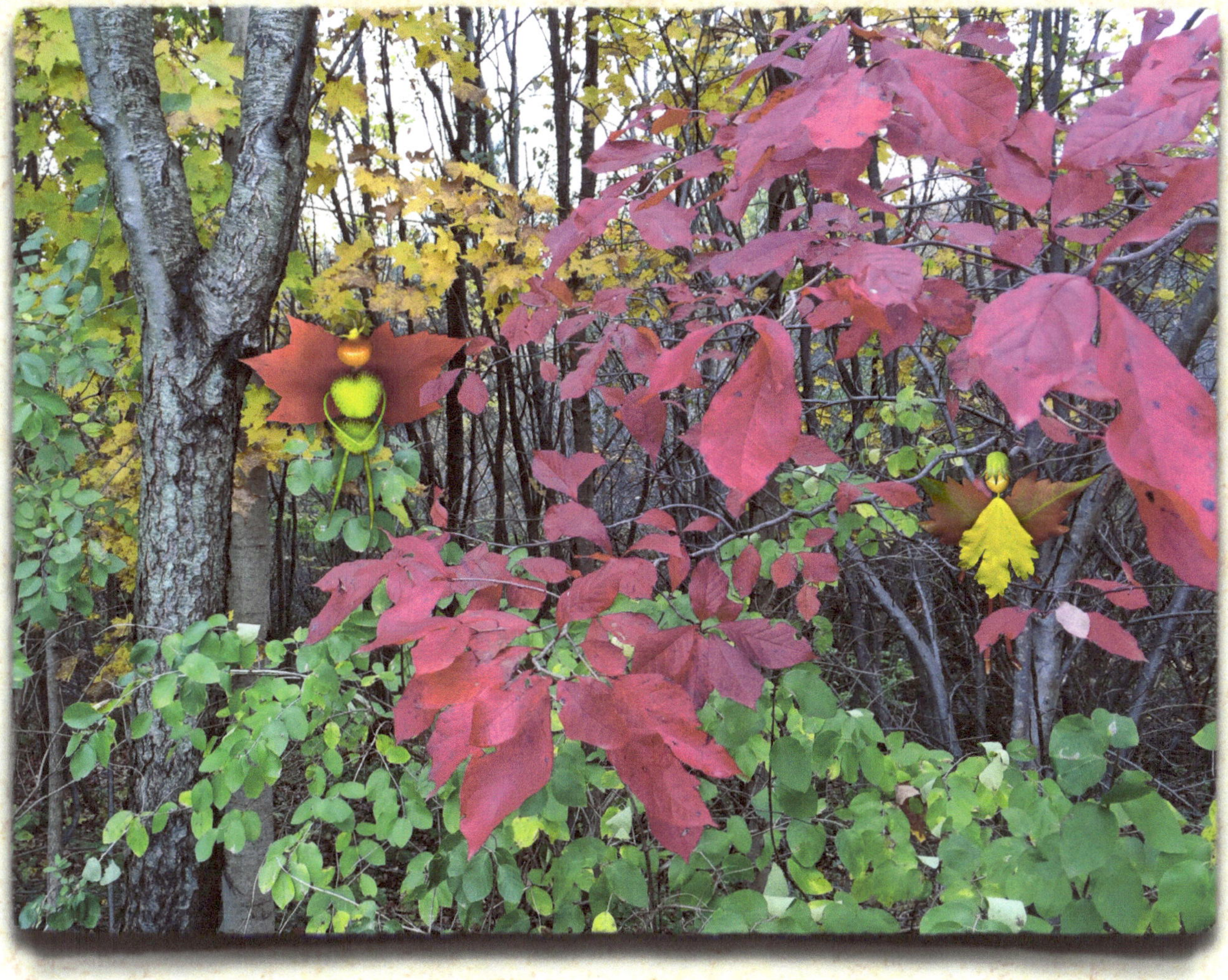

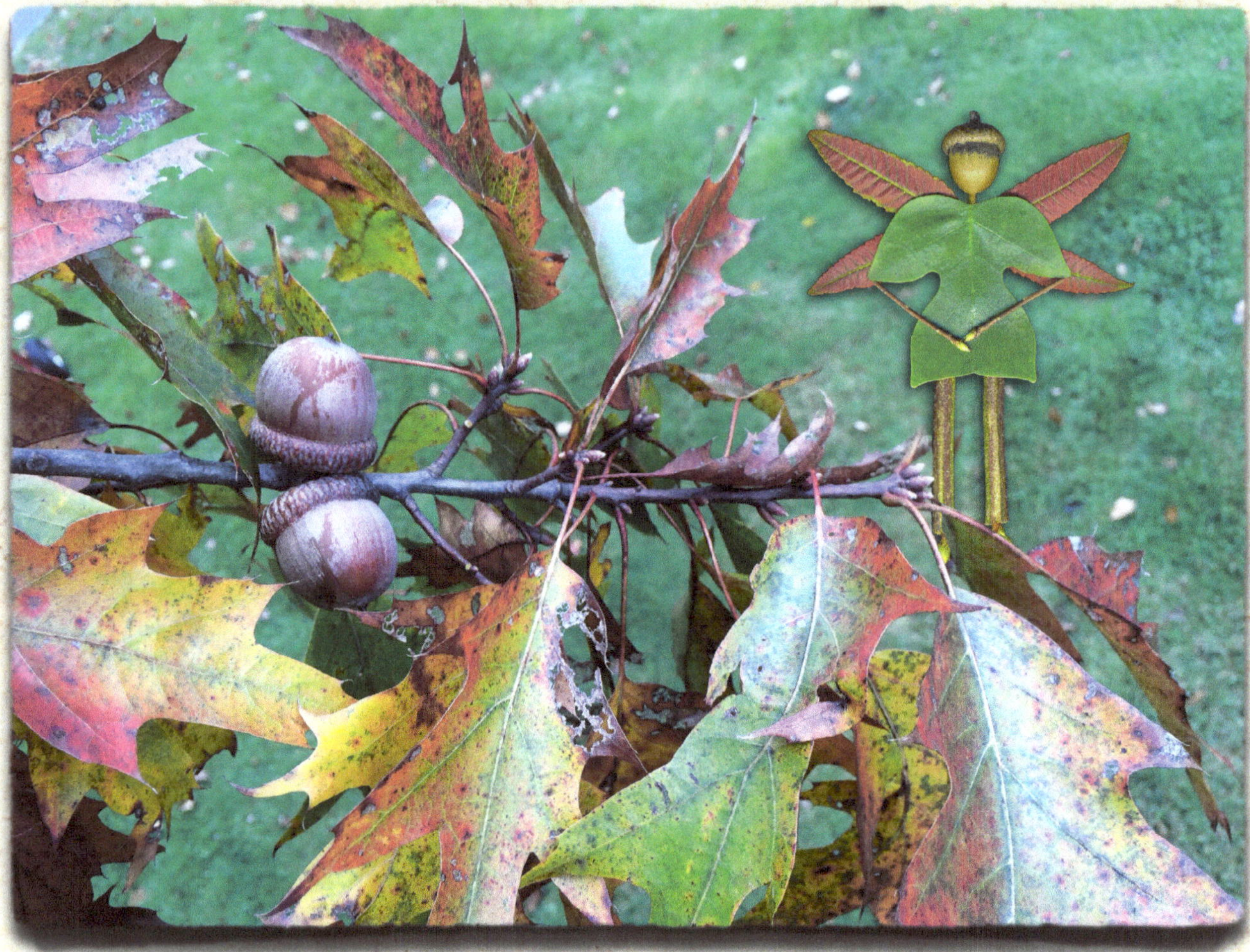

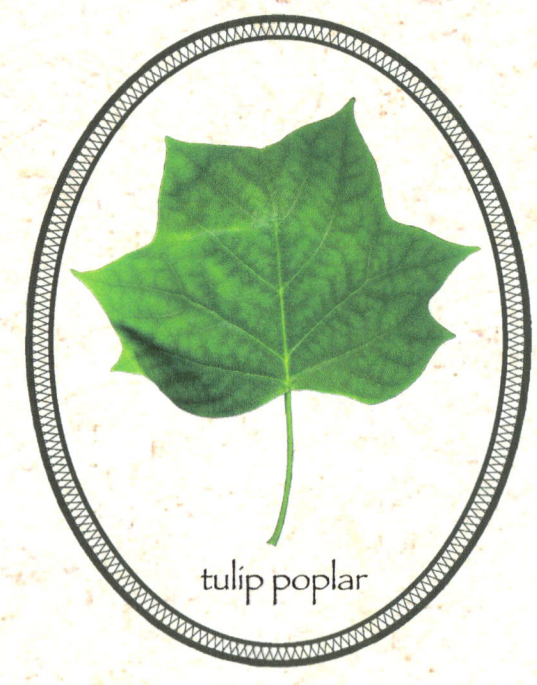

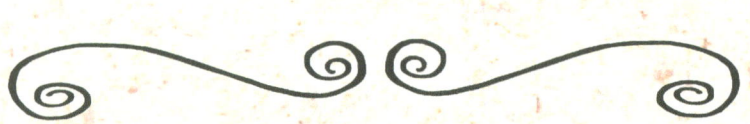

Some leaves keep their bright green hue
till late autumn, then they fall too.

tulip poplar

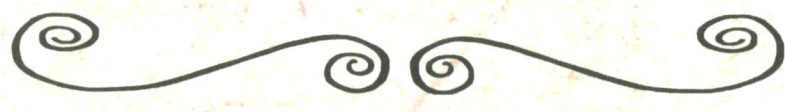

Now all leaves are on the ground,
but fairies still flutter and drift around.

sensitive fern
spore stalks

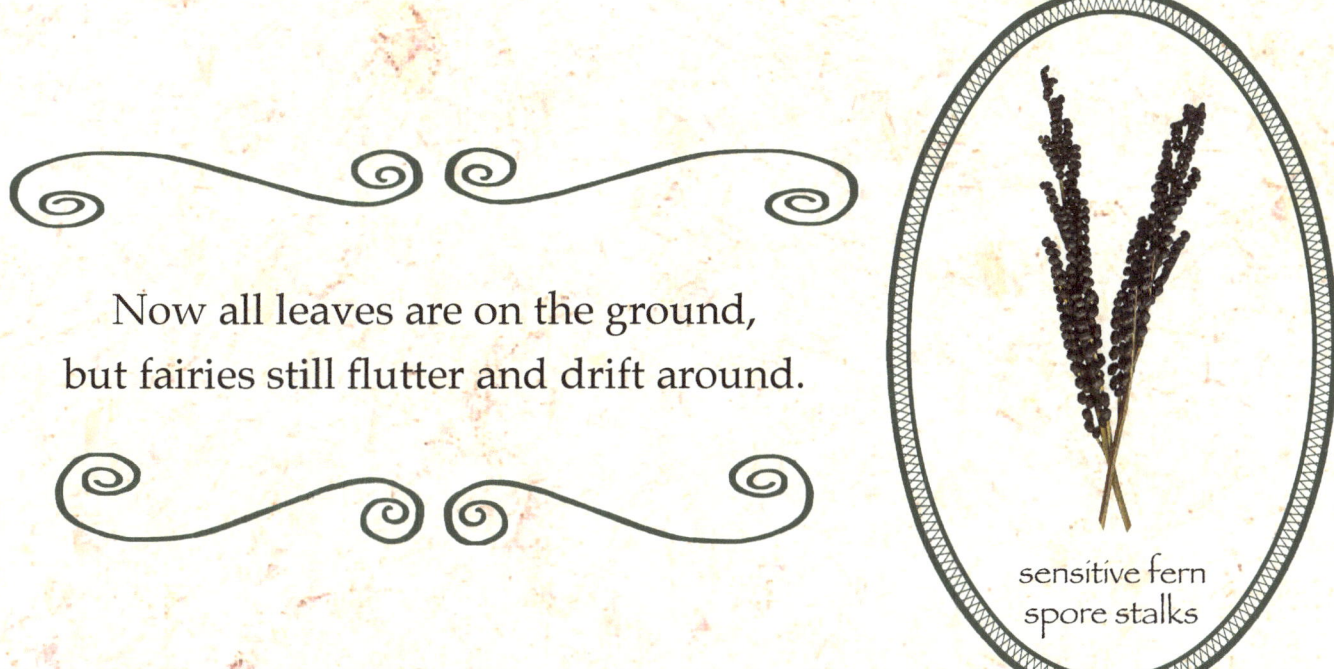

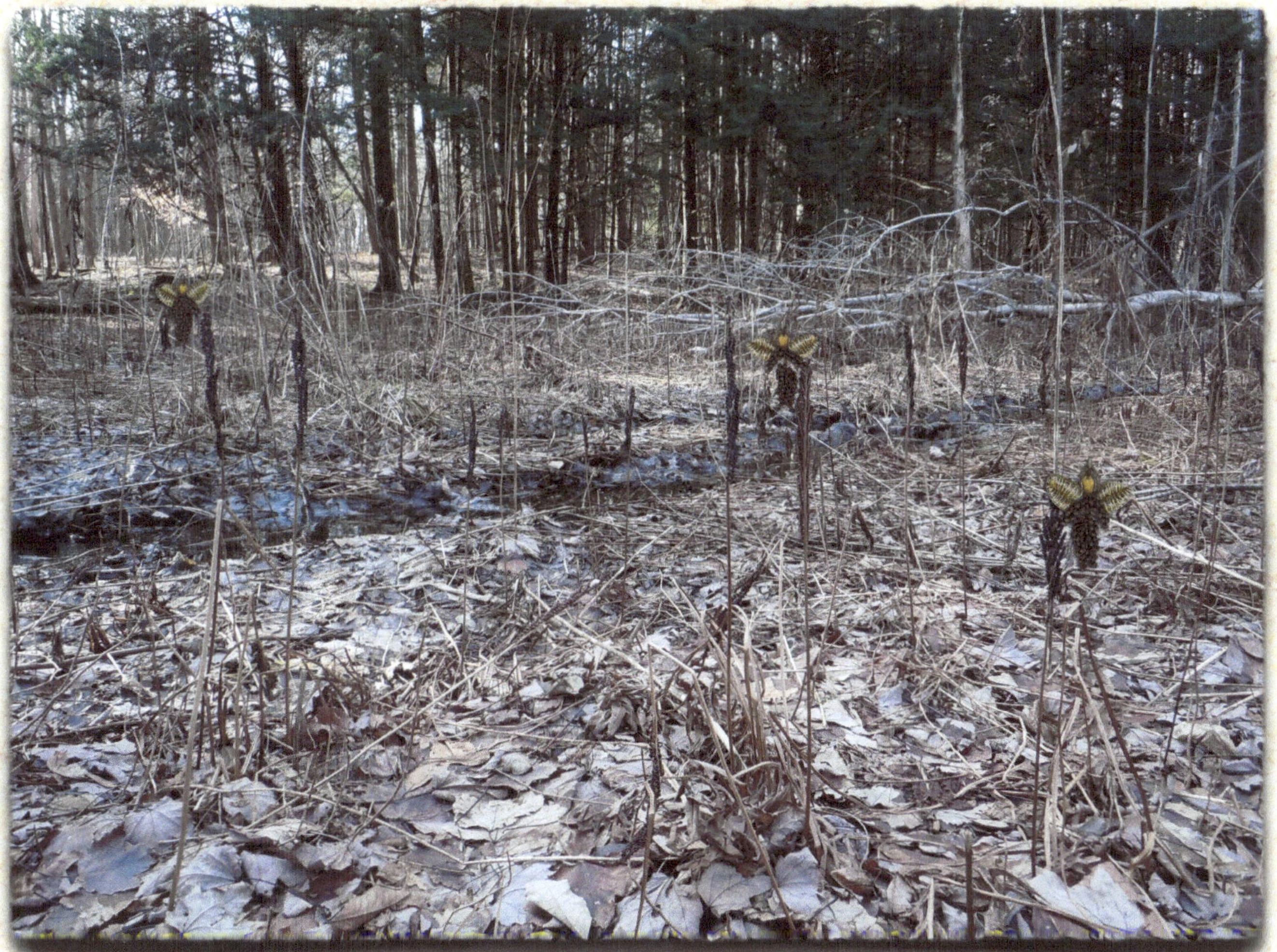

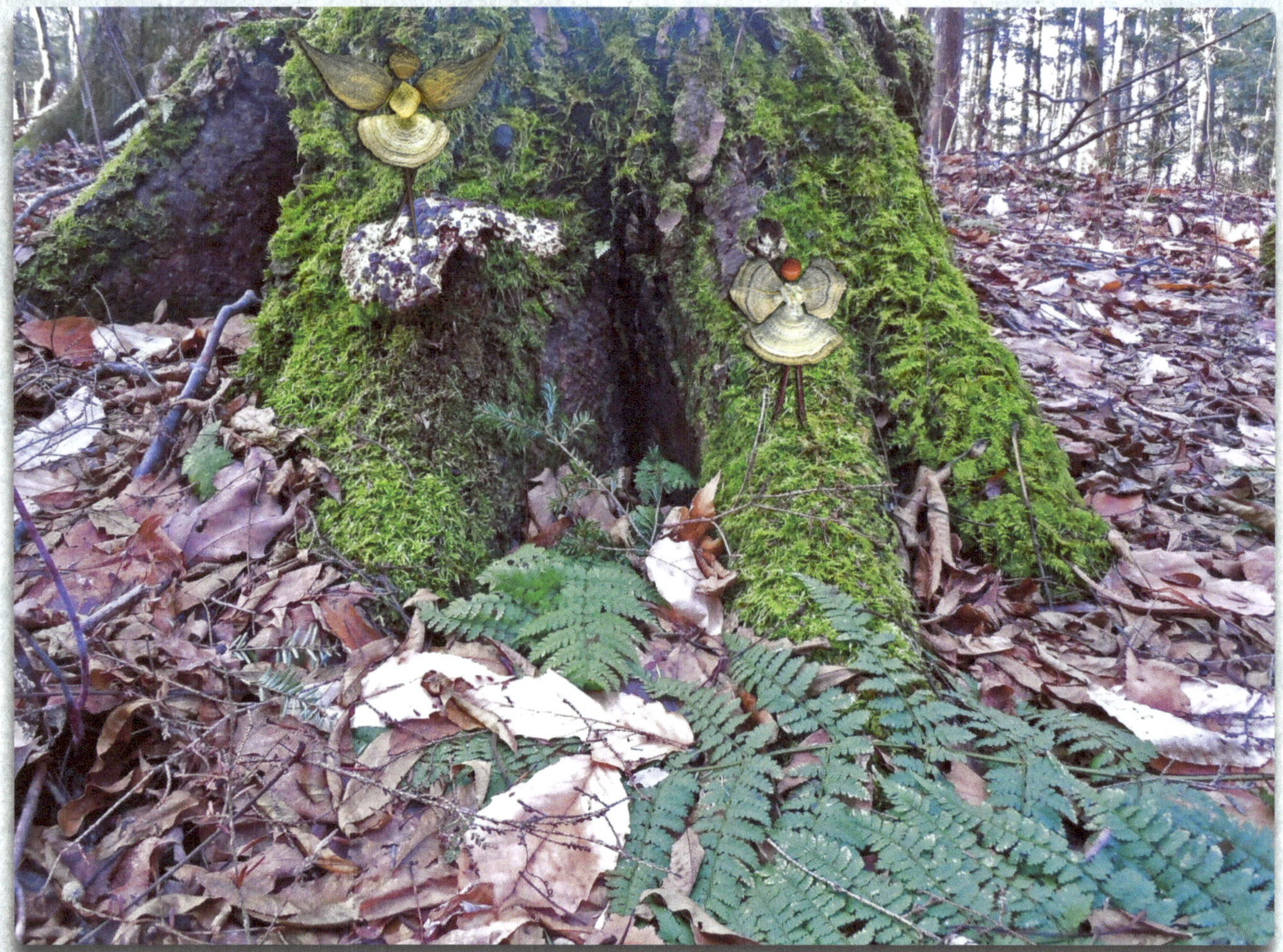

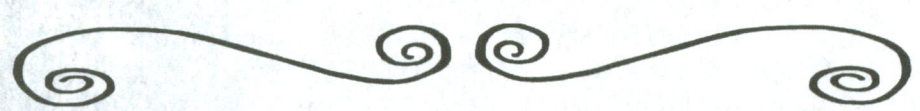

When winter comes, there's still much to see.
Can you spot two on a moss-covered tree?

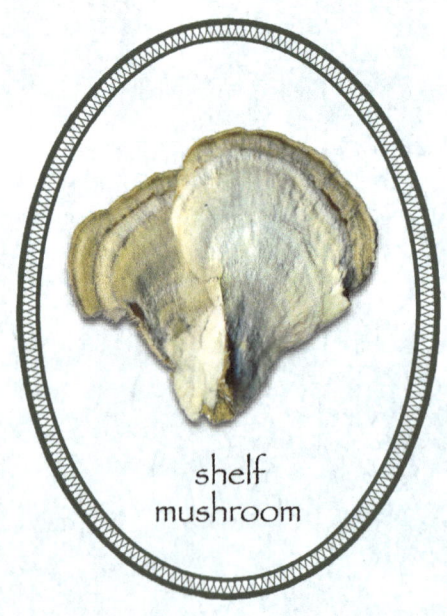

shelf
mushroom

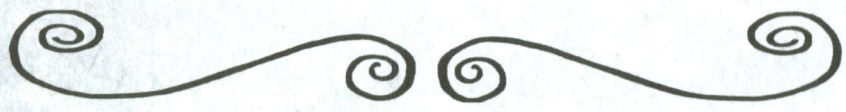

The sun may shine, but cold winds blow.
It won't be long until there's snow.

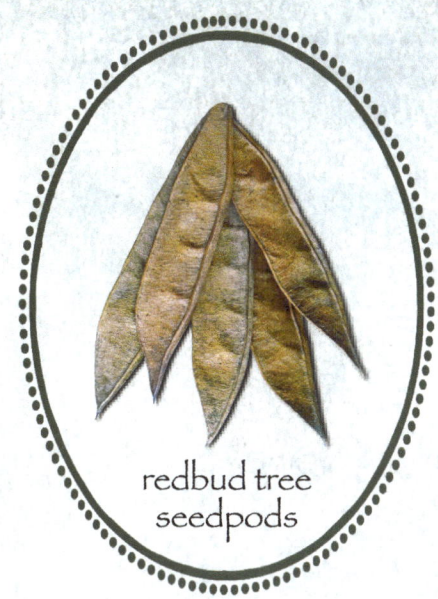

redbud tree
seedpods

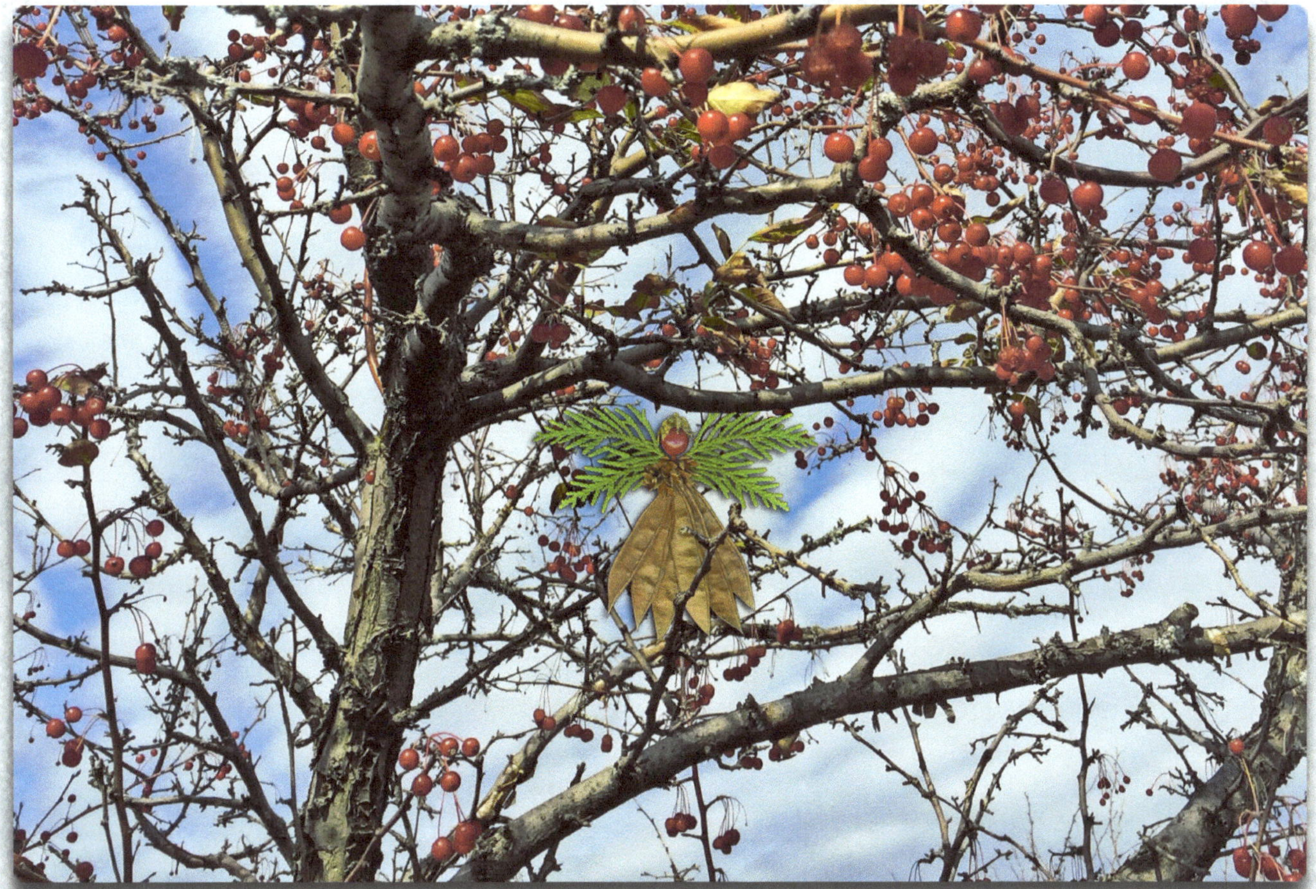

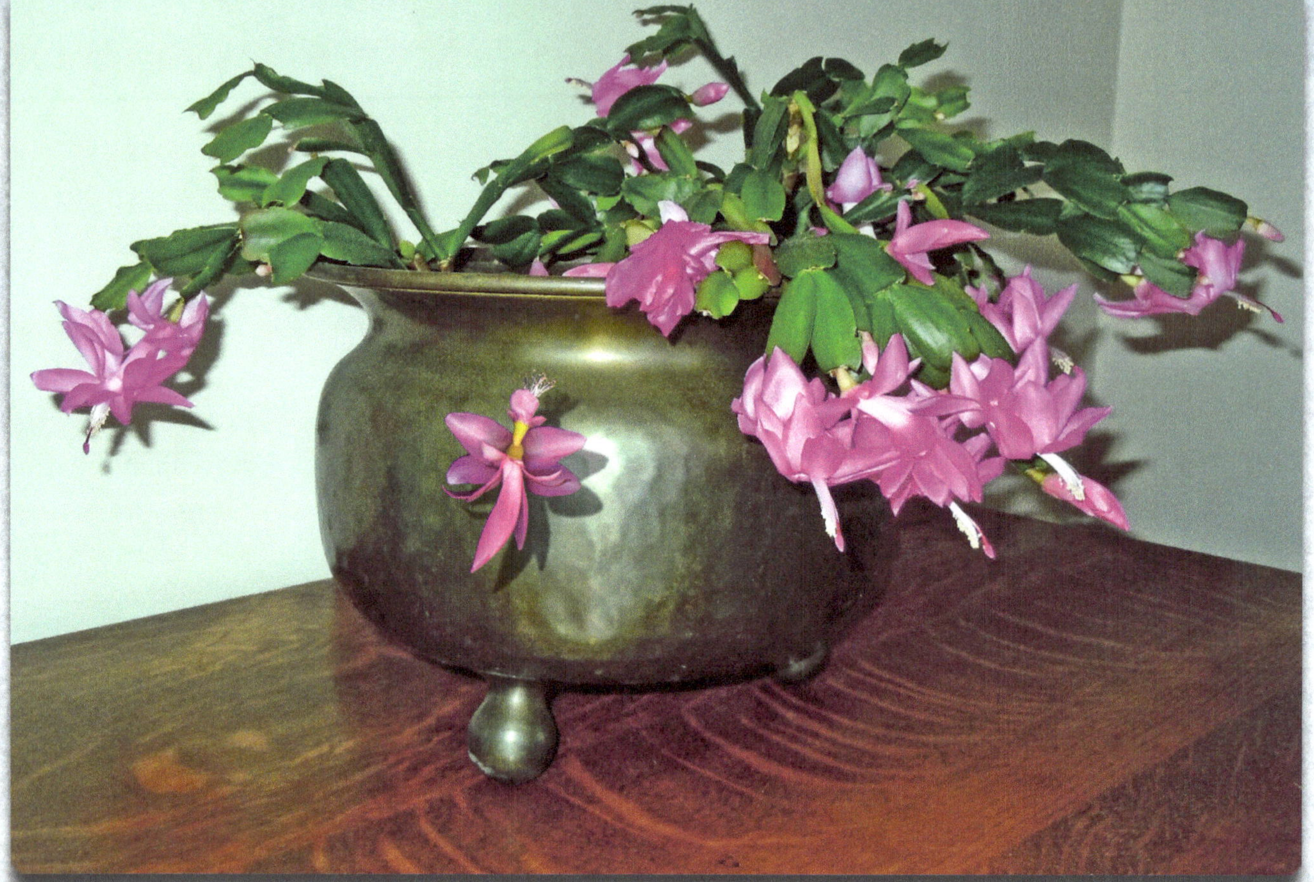

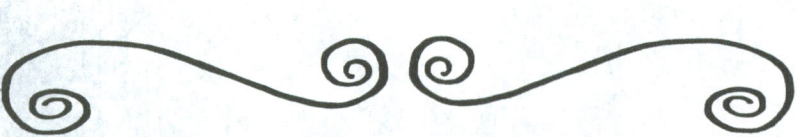

It's too cold for blooms outside,
but not in the house. See what I spied!

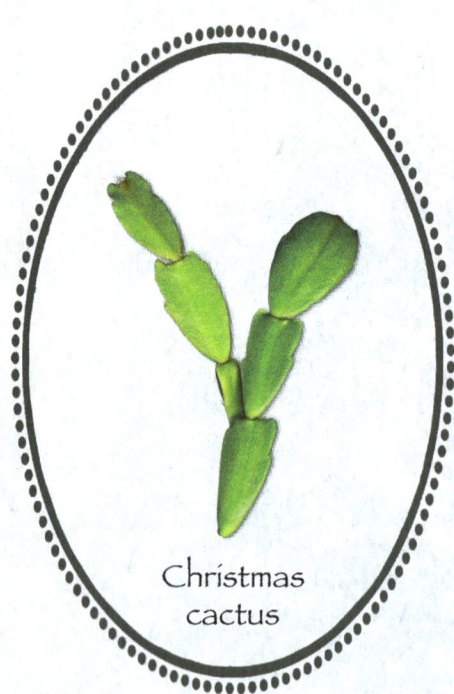

Christmas
cactus

The Old Year Ends
A New Year Begins….

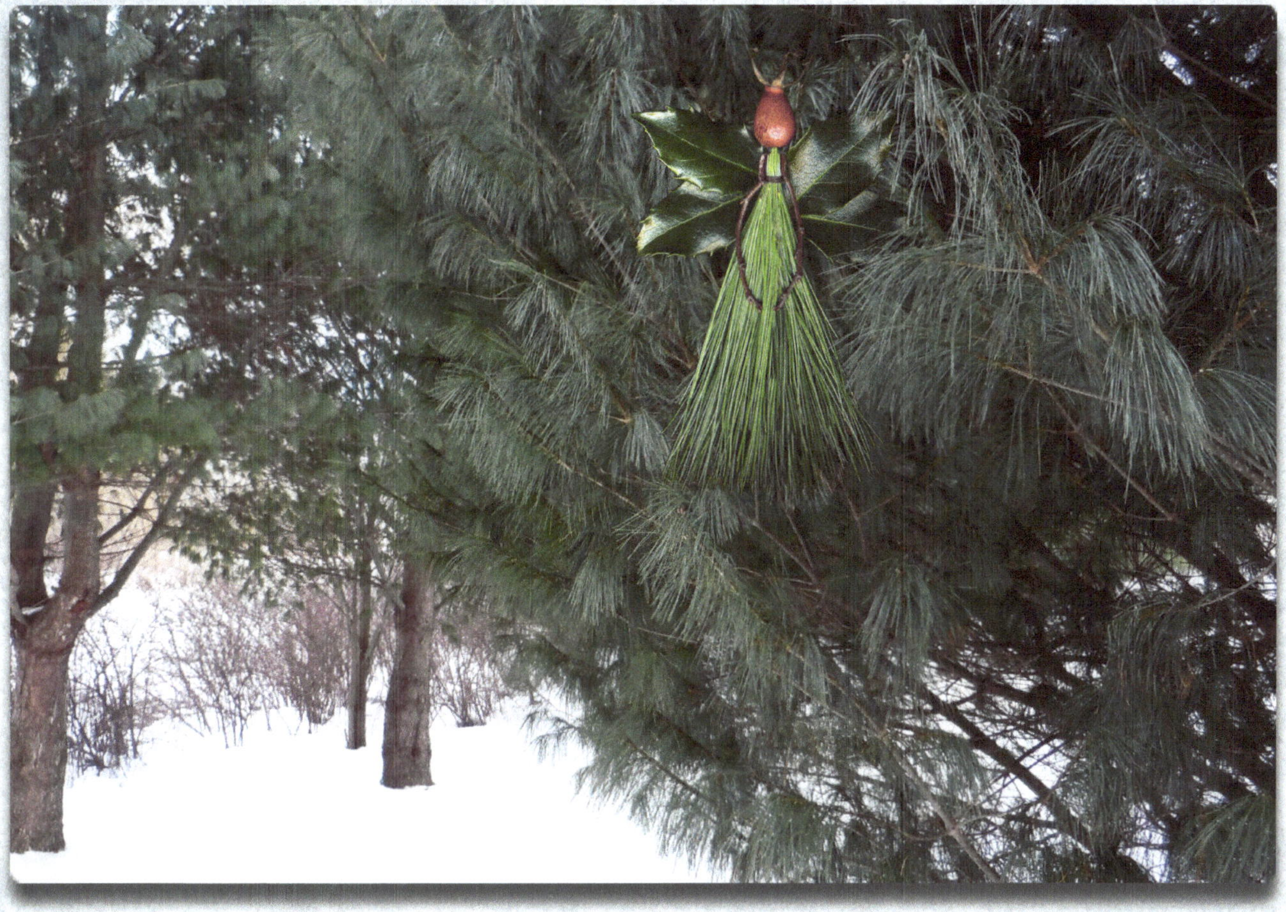

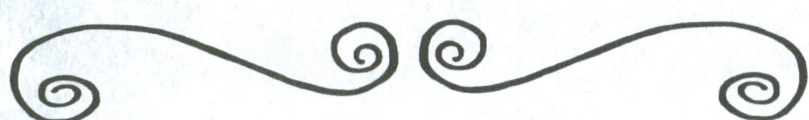

We've gone full cycle but cycles don't end.
Now it's time to start again!

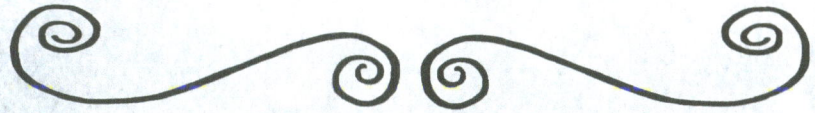

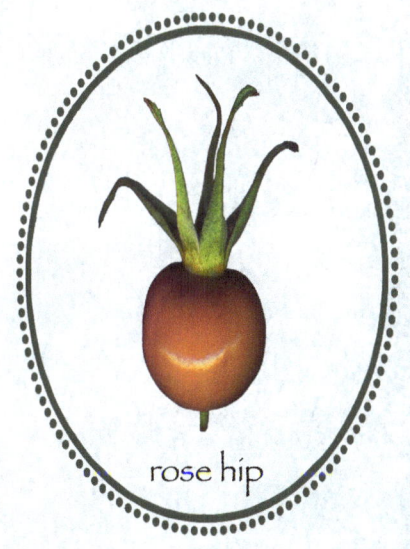

rose hip

Index of plant materials the fairies wear

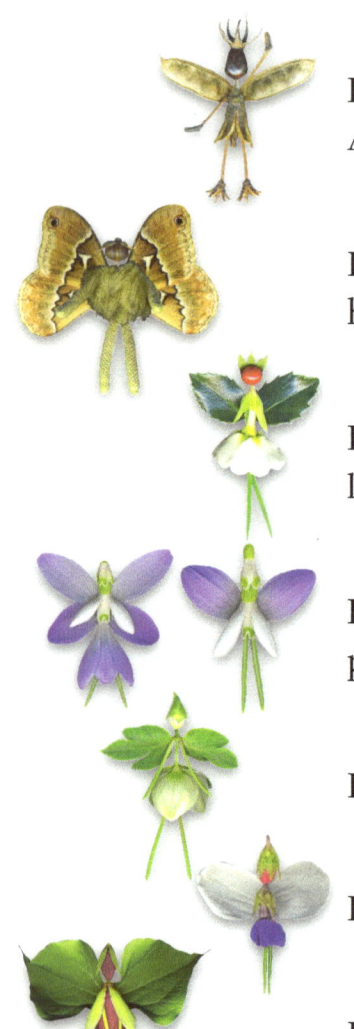

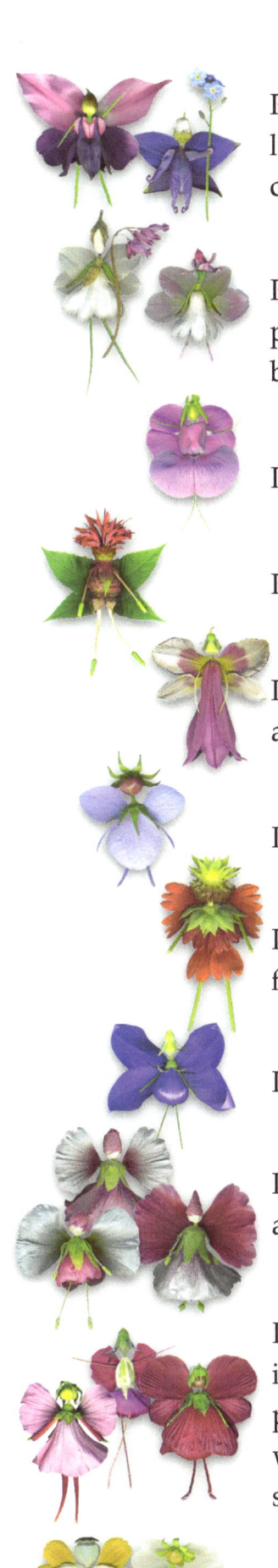

Page 12: parts of a columbine blossom, a glory-of-the-snow seedpod, a lily-of-the-valley blossom, tulip petals, a bleeding heart blossom, and a chive bud and stems

Page 13: the blossoms and bud of a star magnolia bush, white daffodil petals, tulip petals, a single hyacinth seedpod and floret, creeping phlox buds, and crocus leaves.

Page 14: a sweet pea blossom, petals, and tendrils; and a viola seedpod

Page 15: a bee balm blossom, seedhead, and leaves; and lily pistils

Page 16: a trumpet lily blossom, daylily petals, a balloon flower bud, and lily stamens

Page 17: hydrangea petals and stems, and a cosmos bud and calyxes

Page 18: the blossom, petals, seedhead and stems of a burgundy blanket flower

Page 19: petals, buds, and stems of the balloon flower

Page 20 & 21: hollyhock blossoms, buds, and petals; sprigs of lavender, and rosebuds

Page 22: perennial and annual rose mallow blossoms and petals, impatiens stems and seedpods, an uncapped acorn, a hibiscus calyx, parts of four o'clock blossoms, a cosmos bud, a rose campion blossom with its calyx, rose campion petals, a balloon flower bud, and columbine stems

Page 23: a sunflower blossom and petals, part of a Japanese anemone blossom, a poppy seedpod, and a cosmos bud, petals, and stems

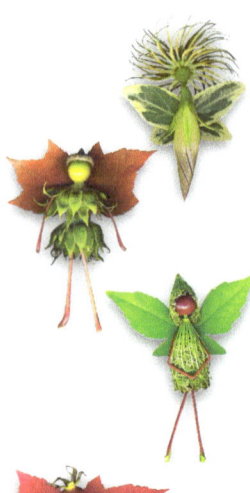

Page 24: a clematis seedhead, a morning glory bud, and eunonymous leaves

Page 25: sunflower seedheads, a rose hip, an acorn cap, maple leaves, and maple leaf stems

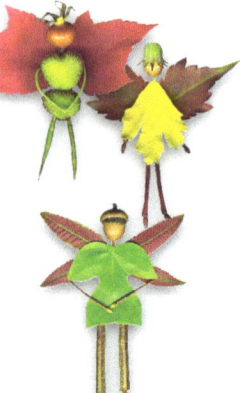

Page 26: Queen Anne's lace seedheads, maple leaf stems, a crab apple and woodland ground cover leaves

Page 27: a rose of Sharon leaf, two different varieties of maple leaves, a crab apple, an African daisy calyx, impatiens stems with seedpods, a rose hip, canna lily seedpods, and cleome seedpods

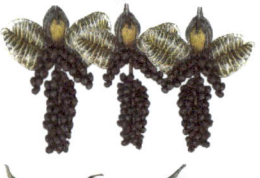

Page 28: a tulip poplar leaf, sunflower stems, azalea stems and buds, an acorn, and sumac leaves

Page 29: sensitive fern spore spikes, rose campion seedpods with weathered calyxes, and weathered daylily seedpods

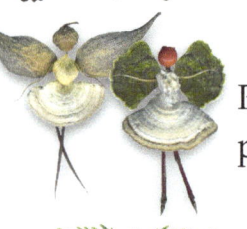

Page 30: shelf-mushrooms, a rose hip, red twigs, spiral grass, milkweed pods, an acorn, dogbane seedpods, and a weathered hydrangea petal

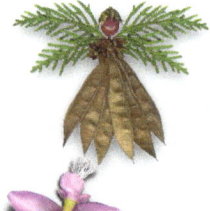

Page 31: American red-bud seedpods, a crab-apple, and cedar twigs with cones

Page 32: all parts of a Christmas cactus flower

Page 33: a rose hip, pine needles, holly leaves, and twigs

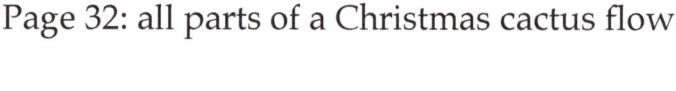

for more information about the art techniques and the artist, visit:
WallflowersAndCards.com

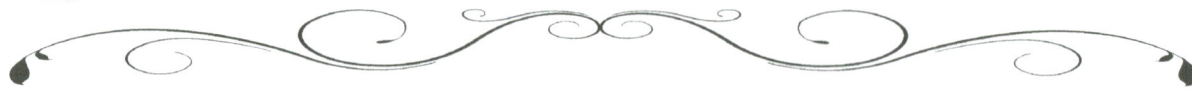